PRAISE FOR *WORKING WHOLE*

"Kourtney has a unique ability to lead you through a self-discovery journey on how to bring purpose and intention to your personal and professional life. She has a commitment to meeting you where you are and guiding you to a place of deeper understanding to more authentically lead, serve, and find joy in your work."

—Amanda Andere

CEO, Funders Together to End Homelessness

"Kourtney is the executive coach that coaches like me depend on to help guide us in our careers. She has the insight of an expert on C-suite leadership coupled with a warmth and humility which are rarely found together."

—Rory Verrett

Managing Partner, Protégé Search
(former Head of Talent Management, NFL)

"There are a lot of career experts out there, but not many that can teach you how to bridge the gap between your spiritual life and your work. Kourtney is an expert guide to help you discover what you are capable of and what it takes to get there."

—Steve Gladis, Ph.D.
Leadership coach and author of
Positive Leadership: The Game Changer at Work

"Kourtney has a deep, spiritual, and lifelong commitment to helping others find inner peace, purpose, and joy. She takes her clients to the depths of who they are, helping them develop and fulfill their life's work."

—Micah Mitchell Hines
Special Counsel, Blackwell Burke (former General Counsel to Minnesota Governor Mark Dayton)

WORKING

WHOLE

WORKING WHOLE

HOW TO UNITE
YOUR SPIRITUAL BELIEFS AND
YOUR WORK TO LIVE FULFILLED

KOURTNEY WHITEHEAD

Disclaimer: Although the examples in this book reflect real-life situations, they are not necessarily descriptions of actual people or organizations but composites drawn from varied contexts.

Requests to publish work from this book should be sent to: kwhitehead@simplyservice.org

Cover and interior design: Sarah Beaudin

Author photo: Photography by Jennifer Beall

ISBN: 978-0-9600419-2-3

To my grandparents—the anchors of my life.

CONTENTS

WHOLE

(hōl)

adjective

1. All of; entire.
2. In an unbroken or undamaged state; in one piece.

noun

1. A thing that is complete in itself.
2. All of something.

YOUR LIFE'S WORK

When you consider your life's work so far, what immediately comes to mind? My hope is that you feel joy and contentment, and motivated to leap out of bed each morning. In my experience as a career coach, however, it often seems that our professional lives are at odds with our personal spiritual beliefs, and this leads many of us to feel disconnected and uninspired by the prospect of work, and groaning at the sound of the alarm each day.

This feeling of being out of place, not working with purpose, often leads us to dreams of retirement, dramatic career changes, or launching new business ventures, and every day I witness these initiating moments of career reflection and transition. We sense that there should be more to life than simply working for achievements or money but are unsure how to find and do more fulfilling work. What I have witnessed in my work over the last 20 years is that while job searches have a clear course of action, following a career path rarely teaches us how to cultivate our best life experience. Despite outward success, I've seen how so many people feel discontented with their work lives and secretly suspect they would be happier if they focused their talents differently. And this discontentment is not only expressed by those struggling in low-paid jobs, or stuck climbing the corporate ladder, but also by the highest-paid CEOs in some of the world's most profitable organizations.

If you too are at that point right now, not knowing where to go next, then it's likely because you want to find greater meaning from the work of your life. Like me, you may have turned to a spiritual practice to seek more peace and joy in your personal life but continue to feel ruled by societal norms in your professional life. Work is often the final piece we seek on the path to spiritual wholeness. It is the last place we choose to bring our spiritual beliefs because in the realm of work, the laws of the human world seem to reign supreme. So, while this book won't tell you how to launch a job search, write a resume, or prepare for an interview, it will show you the actions you need to take *before* you start pursuing your work. And my hope is this book will set you on the path to build a working life that leaves you working whole: working in a way that allows you to bring your spiritual beliefs into your work, and leaves you excited to start each and every new day.

UNITING CORE BELIEFS

For most of us, our professional work occupies a major component of our time on this earth. We spend the bulk of our waking hours engaged in work of some kind. If our spiritual beliefs are truly the guides of our lives, then they also need to be the guides of our careers. The familiar core spiritual beliefs of surrender, gratitude, love, power, and so on, are found at the heart of almost all spiritual paths and traditions, and outline how we should think, feel, and behave in an ideal spiritual state. But how do we use them to negotiate real-world obstacles, like a boss you do not trust or a job you feel stuck in?

In the following chapters, I want to share how to bring these beliefs into your work to reach a deeper level of satisfaction by working and living anchored in what you believe. By focusing on making eight core spiritual beliefs actionable, you will be able to use them to gain clarity, inspiration, and direction on what your next work steps should be. Taking the time to integrate what you believe into your work life will stop you from making, perhaps, yet another short-term career decision striving

Matching our lives to what we believe can be so daunting that we may dismiss the possibility of ever achieving wholeness where our spiritual and our human lives are completely joined.

toward the wrong long-term goals. Of course, there are many forks along the paths that determine our ability to listen for and follow a work calling. These decisions are what you can own and influence. The goal of this book is to help you recognize the questions and choices that matter most.

CHASING HAPPINESS

In contrast to living whole, pursuing happiness feels more actionable. When we think about the things that make us happy, we are likely to envision something tangible and achievable. Happiness goals are something we can pursue every day. Perhaps your happiness is triggered by a person, a food, an event, a place, or goal. You may link finding a new love interest or getting in better physical shape with future happiness. You may not have the happiness goal just yet, but you already have a clear sense of how to pursue it. These goals are not lofty lifetime spiritual pursuits; they are daily quests guided by our immediate desires.

Think about how easy it is to be happy about a new love interest or a new job. That is even the case with a new car or a new wardrobe, as they fill us with a sense of possibility for what *could* be. Wanting to feel happy is a natural pursuit. The problem is that we tend to be so preoccupied with pursuing desires that will only return momentary happiness that we don't have enough energy left to focus on the things that will provide us with steady and sustainable joy. We are too busy trying to be happy to actually achieve it consistently which can leave us trapped in a cycle of pursuing "new," "next," and "more."

I know this cycle well and it is exhausting and painful to endure. I was happy in fleeting moments but spent most of my time desiring more and feeling disappointed with what I had. I was ashamed of how I felt. As a spiritual person, I knew I was failing to live in the peace and joy of my beliefs, and also failing to find meaning in my life experience. Of course, I kept this a secret from most of the world. If you knew me during these times, you would have thought I was thriving spiritually while achieving professional success. Instead, with the acquisition of each new thing, person, or job, it became harder and harder to be satisfied.

Many of us start to lose hope in contented living and turn our frustration inward. As we find it more difficult to satisfy our need for happiness, we begin to secretly fear that we will never be satisfied. We may even begin to fear that the problem is not our choices, but a personality flaw embedded deep within us. We may even question that our spiritual beliefs are flawed. But the problem is not inside us. Instead, the problem is that we are not taught what it actually takes to achieve fulfilled living. We are taught what it takes to pursue a career. And, unless you plan to work as a religious or spiritual teacher, we have to reconcile two worlds that often seem unrelated—our beliefs and our work—in order to find a sustainable source of joy.

BELIEFS: THE WELL OF FULFILLMENT

Think about it another way: If you were trapped on a deserted island with only one item, would you rather have a bucket or a well?

The bucket is quite useful, if you can find a source of drinkable water. But, will you ever find water and how long will it take? The well is an immediate source of drinkable water, but you'll have to figure out how to get the water out of it. Both tasks require ingenuity and effort, but which pursuit is the better use of your time?

Spending time looking for jobs that will make you happy by trial and error is like choosing the bucket. It could work someday by sheer luck, but it could also be an endless pursuit. It could leave you seeking forever and never quenching your thirst. The well, on the other hand, is a known source of drinkable water and focusing on how to get the water out of the well is a much better use of your time. With the well, you know that quenching your thirst is possible if you stay committed to the task at hand.

Our spiritual beliefs represent the well that holds joy and fulfillment. We know that sustainable happiness sits within the well of the spiritual. But instead of choosing the well, we spend most of our work lives wandering around in the world with our bucket hoping to stumble upon fulfillment. The power of our beliefs to set us free from this cycle is exactly why we are drawn to religion and spiritual pursuits in massive numbers.

This is not a religious book. I will leave you to explore religious doctrine questions for yourself in the spiritual practice that most resonates with you, so while I use the word "God," please substitute this for your preferred term or tradition. The sole purpose of this book is to teach you *how* your spiritual beliefs can transform and amplify the work of your life.

HOW TO USE THIS BOOK

William Shakespeare famously compared life to a play and us as actors on a stage, and one of the values of the creative arts is that they can show us an entirely different reality. But we are going to take a more modern approach and throughout I'll be asking you to create a metaphorical TV show with your life. The purpose of this metaphor is to depict how your life experience is shaped by your beliefs, and to illustrate your role in creating the show you want to be living and working in. To create your ideal show, you'll need to play the role of producer, writer, and actor in order to illustrate the work that you have to do to create a meaningful life. Don't worry, I'll be with you for every decision point along the way.

So in Part I we'll focus on integrating a core set of universal beliefs—humility, surrender, discipline, gratitude, connection, love, power, and patience—and how each one shapes our thinking and builds life experiences that will lead to our work callings. We'll then use our spiritual beliefs to guide the kind of show and episodes we can produce. We'll imagine the script our spiritual beliefs would create for our lives. You'll find that exploring these beliefs will challenge you to consider how putting each belief into action daily impacts your work and your ability to be who you authentically are. And by the end of Part I, you will have answered important questions about your beliefs and assessed how well you have integrated them into your life. You will also have a framework to use in making life and career decisions—big and small.

Part II addresses how our beliefs impact the way we show up in the world, what we get done, and the role work plays in our spiritual practice. It explores who we are supposed to be, where we are supposed to be, and the value of our time in this life. And we'll decipher what impact that show's script has on your character and how an actor would play the role. By the end of this section, you'll be ready to assess and make tangible changes, which will prepare you to listen for, and follow, your work callings.

> **NOTE**
>
> Almost all of the chapter topics are ideas that others have written entire books on. We are going to cover a lot of spiritual and work-related content rather quickly. This book is organized in short chapters that will only scratch the surface of many topics. The priority is understanding the overall framework so that you can use your beliefs to do your highest and most meaningful work. You will find journaling exercises throughout the book to support you in exploring your unique feelings and intentions on each topic, but I also recommend seeking other resources and teachings to reflect further on any chapter you feel you need more time with.

Finally, go slow. Making your beliefs actionable requires significant periods of reflection, growth, and life experience. It is not enough to read this book. You will have to consciously assess where you stand today and implement change into your life. Try not to rush the process or digest the material too quickly. The promise of your highest work is worth any extra time it might take to get there.

That's the plan for our time together. Your work awaits, so let's get started.

PART I

INTEGRATED

in•te•grate (in(t)ə͵grāt)

verb

1. Combine (one thing) with another so that they become a whole. Past tense: integrated; 3rd person present: integrates; present participle: integrating.

CHAPTER 1

HUMILITY

Humility is our belief in the miraculous worth of every soul. Being humble means that we are aware of the equality between our value when compared to another. It reduces our need to compete for self-importance because we know what our true value is as a spiritual being, and this has huge implications on the life we lead and the work we pursue.

A CONFLICTING BELIEF

Fully embracing humility in our work lives can be challenging and potentially career inhibiting. After all, most hiring managers will say they value humility in their employees, and yet consistently select candidates skilled in self-promotion over those that are humbler in their description of their abilities and accomplishments. In fact, your "executive presence"—how quickly your verbal and non-verbal communication style translates into an employer's trust in your ability to be a leader—can often be the difference between landing a job or not.

Of course, bias (especially racial, age, and gender) and cultural dynamics also factor into the assessment of a candidate's executive presence, as do subtler things, such as body language, tone, and word usage because they are deemed to show strength and confidence. Focusing on "what makes us better than others" helps us shape others' perception and succeed in the workplace—which is why being comfortable with self-promotion is so frequently correlated with landing a big job or getting promoted.

In contrast, humility may lead a candidate to express their views with less emphasis on the role they played in a situation. The humble candidate is more likely to use the word "we" instead of "I" when describing achievements; to see the impact of their work as a team effort; or acknowledge the influence of circumstances beyond their control. Humble responses might cause the interviewer to question whether this candidate has the ability to lead in a particular culture.

Embracing humility and being perceived as "confident" or "successful" is the first of many conflicts we may run into when trying to integrate our spiritual beliefs into our work lives.

THE QUESTION:
INTEGRATING HUMILITY

So, do we really want to live in humility at all times? Is that even a good idea at work? Many of us have spent our lives working on our identity, self-esteem, and confidence. I know I've had to work very hard at it. Why are we pushing ourselves to acquire and accomplish more, if not to elevate our status? Why would our spiritual beliefs want us to lower our view of ourselves if that makes the world perceive us as weaker or less capable?

Humility is at the foundation of all spiritual practices and yet, for some of the reasons already explored, it can be a difficult belief to integrate into our everyday lives. For this reason, the question we'll be reflecting on in this chapter is:

Q: Is my belief in humility integrated into my life?

To start to answer that question, we'll also need to explore:

- What do we believe about humility?
- Why is humility spiritually important?
- Is humility relevant to our work lives?
- Do we need humility to live in fulfillment?

Now take a look at the following statement. Is this what you believe about humility? Would you say this statement is true or false for you?

I believe that my soul is a magnificent and divine gift. My soul is no greater nor lesser than anyone else's, and I am most fulfilled when I am awake to my soul's presence and aware of its permanent equality to all other souls.

There are two things we must believe for this statement to be true. The first is about the soul's existence and the second is about its equal status. As you consider whether this is what you believe, think about whether you believe that all souls are gifts from God or sacred in some way. I'm not talking about your personality, or the things that make up your identity, but your soul—the spiritual aspect of human existence.

The Hindi phrase *Namaste* has now become part of Western culture. We might hear it said at the end of a yoga class or see it on a social media post. *Namaste* can be translated as "The spirit in me bows to the spirit in you." The phrase is a greeting or closing that recognizes and honors that we all share a common and sacred gift which is our soul. The soul gives us life and cannot be explained fully by science or fabricated by man. It is your life force deep inside of you right now that is hoping this book will bring you closer to God and the work you are meant to do with your life.

EXERCISE

Grab your journal and spend a few moments mulling over the following questions:

· Do you believe that your soul actually exists outside of your ego or individual personhood?

· Is your soul a beautiful and sacred gift?

SOUL EQUALITY

This gets us to the next question: Do you believe that your soul is equal to all others?

If your soul is equal to all others, then it is free to live in humility. There is no one with a soul more valuable than yours, and that includes presidents, kings, movie stars, and even Oprah. Your soul doesn't have to strive and push for self-importance. It already has it. If you believe that your soul is equal to all others, then you also believe in the spiritual value of living in humility and that you are most fulfilled when you embrace it.

Integrating humility into our work lives will take us to different, more adventurous places because we will be spiritually secure enough to attempt those journeys.

Holding a belief is easy. What's harder is integrating that belief into our everyday lives. Yet that is where our beliefs were always meant to be used. A belief in humility takes us past our need to strive and push for self-importance. It is the belief that can halt our instinct to run from bold assignments for fear of being found lacking or insignificant. Our ability to integrate humility into our life has profound implications on our work.

Living in humility connects us to our soul, but what does that mean on a day-to-day basis? How are we expected to behave if we have integrated humility into our lives?

YOUR SHOW

To explore that question, let's turn our attention to creating our metaphorical TV show. So, let's start by imagining we are creating a new Netflix series, called *Earth Is the New Green* or *13 Reasons to Live*.

The first step in any creation is critical. Which question you find hardest in this book will depend on your unique circumstances and life experiences. For some, choosing to integrate their beliefs will be the largest challenge. For others, choosing to rearrange their life to pursue their work callings will pose the bigger obstacle. Either way, I think it would be fair to say that answering the following questions will form the basis of one of the most important decisions you can make.

- What is your show supposed to be about based on your spiritual beliefs?

- What role should your character play and how important are they?

Here are two possible show ideas. I have lived them both. As you read each one, reflect on which most portrays your thoughts and actions. In other words: *Which show are you living in right now?*

SCENARIO 1:

13 REASONS TO LIVE—STARRING MY CHARACTER

- **Plot setting:** Exploring my surroundings and living my life.
- **Theme:** The plight of my well-being, goals, desires, and frustrations.
- **Pilot episode:** My birth.
- **Series' conflicts:** Am I safe? Am I sad? Am I good enough? Am I loved? What do I want? Am I happy yet?
- **Finale episode:** My death.
- **Characters:** Clearly, I was the main character, while my inner circle of family, friends, and colleagues played the supporting roles. Extras were played by anyone else I came across but didn't move *my* storyline forward. These characters hung out in the background and were more a part of the *setting* than actual characters. Like most shows with a clear protagonist, there had to be an antagonist (or two or groups of people).

At different times of your life, your antagonist(s) might be a family member, an ex-lover, a former friend, a boss, a coworker, a government, political entity, or demographic. In my case it was my own alter ego that sabotaged my progress.

- **My character's role:** To search for happiness and advance my storyline. My character was there to think about and try to live my best life. I was there to try and address my series' conflicts.

SCENARIO 2:

EARTH IS THE NEW GREEN—STARRING EVERYBODY

- **Plot setting:** Exploring Earth and the life that inhabits it.
- **Theme:** The plight of all living beings with diverse, but equally important, storylines happening concurrently.
- **Pilot episode:** The beginning of time.
- **Series' conflicts:** Humanity's struggles with themselves and each other. Humanity's impact on other living beings. Humanity's spiritual awakening.
- **Finale episode:** The end of time.
- **Characters:** Every living being. All characters play an equal role in the show. No main characters, no supporting characters, no extras. No protagonists or antagonists.

- **My role:** To develop my character's role in the series' conflicts and play my part well within the season the show is covering my lifespan. To fully appreciate the limited time, I have to be in front of the camera.

Despite being raised with religion, I have spent most of my life living the first version of the show. I thought my purpose as a living being was to pursue happiness and my mind was consumed with things that related to my own well-being. I didn't see anything wrong with this, as I also tried to be kind to others and helpful. It wasn't that I was selfish in my behavior, as much as I was self-focused with my thoughts and orientation toward life.

I was rarely aware of how that self-focus impacted my actions. When I was aware, I justified it as normal human preoccupation. I didn't hold myself accountable for integrating my life with my belief in humility, though if you asked me about it I would have said I believed I was humble.

I thought that by talking less, making self-effacing comments, or being a good team player, I could demonstrate humility—even when my mind, heart, and life were reflecting a disconnect.

Now don't get me wrong, I cared deeply about my supporting characters. But I rarely had time to fully appreciate the beauty of their souls because I was too consumed with my own experience. Their characters were an important part of *my* show, but I wasn't reflecting the equal value of all souls.

Truthfully, there were things I liked about my version of the show. On the one hand, I was under a lot of pressure to search for my own happiness. There was a constant need for conflict with my desires and frustrations to keep my storyline interesting. Yet, I was a main character in the show. The main focus was on my experience. So, in my world at least, I felt special.

In contrast, living the spiritual belief of humility called me to be living in the second version. It is the show where I am a character, but no more important than any other. There is less pressure when the expectations of my impact on the show are lower. But that also means that I feel less special. I enjoyed feeling special and it was (and still is at times) hard for me to let go of those self-focused tendencies.

Deciding to move past the thinking that places you as the main character is key to integrating humility in your everyday life. Self-focus can be a match that lights a host of distracting and counter-productive thoughts and desires. I spent an enormous amount of time thinking and rethinking ways to move my story forward and get what I wanted, instead of engaging with life tangibly. Compulsive self-focus is a distraction that will derail your efforts to find and do meaningful work every time.

Too much self-focus can keep us trapped in a version of our show that will never lead us to fulfillment and our highest work.

CHOOSING A NEW EXPERIENCE

It may seem like a simple analogy, but these two shows represent how most of us experience life. Right now, each of us is living in one or the other of these shows. Our orientation toward the world is the life we are producing. One of these shows is already playing in our minds and limiting or manifesting our work.

The essence of living in humility is in choosing to produce the second version of the show, and if we want to live humility (or any belief for that matter) we have to start with how we think about that belief: how we think about our own importance in relation to others. We have to consider the question: What sort of thoughts did a show with me as the main character cultivate? What I found is that life as a main character was incredibly time-consuming because it kept my thoughts focused on my needs and desires, for example:

- The best or a better life partner
- Things I didn't have
- My favorite foods
- A more uplifted emotional state
- More exciting experiences
- New accomplishments
- More power and influence
- Erotic adventures
- More money or material gains

And probably my *most* time-consuming thoughts were about changing the present moment, which included just about anything I could put the word "too" in front of. The list was endless, but here are a few that immediately came to mind.

- I'm too tired.
- It's too early.
- It's too late.
- My hair is too frizzy.
- My skin is too oily.
- It is too hot outside.
- It is too cold outside.
- My thighs are too big.
- My job is too boring.
- My job doesn't pay enough.
- My stomach is not flat enough.
- My husband is not affectionate enough.
- My friends or family are not supportive enough.

Now these desires or dislikes may all have been legitimate assessments of my situation. The problem is that giving myself an elevated "special" status oriented my perspective to place too much attention on my own experience. Once focused squarely on my experience (which will never be perfect), I didn't have the capacity to think about the things that actually lead me to fulfillment. In other words, I was wasting my time and potential on possibly unreachable desires and petty annoyances. My attention would have been better used by shifting the focus to living my spiritual beliefs where true fulfillment could be found.

YOUR CHOICE:
TO STEP OUT OF THE SPOTLIGHT

Religious traditions anchor in humility because before you can rebuild a burning house, you first have to put out the fire. Humility puts out the mental fires and emotional dramas that drive time-sucking and ever-distracting thoughts of insecurities, expectations, frustrations, and desires.

Humility may be a belief you are already living for the most part. When you read the description of the two shows, you may clearly see your perspective aligned with the show about everyone. If so, you're ahead of the game. If not, you have the spiritual choice to integrate what you believe about humility into your life. You can do this by becoming more aware of when your mind tries to make you the main character by placing your desires and frustrations at the center of your thoughts. Then work to choose to change the channel to the new show.

By consciously noticing when you are living in the first show, you will slowly create a new version of the show in your mind—one that leaves you with the capacity to look around outside of your own experience.

HUMILITY: THE TRANSFORMER

The life you create is the fruit of your thoughts, but what kind of fruit do humble thoughts produce? And will that lead to greater fulfillment and meaningful work?

Humility transforms your relationship with yourself, but it also transforms your relationship with everyone else you come in contact with. Because instead of living with the idea that people can have special status, humility grants you a safe, solid, permanent status of *equal* rank. In the show with humility, there are neither extras nor lesser characters. There are no people there only to be fixed or rescued by you, the main character. In every circumstance, your character is no greater than any other. If you compare yourself to someone who is struggling to regain their sanity—perhaps living in poverty or fighting substance addiction—you harbor no feelings of superiority over them. Even in helping or supporting them, you can do that with an honest connection because you feel no separation between the rank of your soul and theirs.

There is neither a main character nor celebrity guest. There are no characters with greater fan appeal or focus. In every circumstance, your character is no lesser than *any* other. If you compare yourself to someone who is recognized for their rare talents—who perhaps has extraordinary wealth or who holds a position of high power—you harbor no feelings of inferiority toward them. Even in helping or supporting them, you can do so with an honest connection because you feel no separation between your rank in humanity and theirs.

The gift of integrating humility into your work life is that, when we are free from the pressure to be "special," we are also free from the fear of being found "flawed" or "insignificant."

The humble you can be kind and patient with your flaws and the flaws of others, and this is a game changer in the workplace. You will be a loyal coworker and a more supportive leader. You are also able to accept whatever your life circumstances may be at the moment—be that accomplished or struggling. This gives you the ability to ride the ups and downs of a career.

No significant goal has a straight upward trajectory and your ability to integrate humility into your work life will give you the resilience to stay the course. The humble you will be comfortable and confident when working with individuals at any level. You are less likely to be intimidated by superiors and are able to add value as a thought leader and peer despite title differences.

When we are truly humble, our confidence comes authentically from being connected to our soul. We are better listeners and can assess a situation with a more attentive view. We are better strategists because we think through implications well outside of ourselves. We are more effective business people and leaders. And our executive presence doesn't suffer from bringing a spiritual belief in humility into our work—it stems from it. We are able to exude a natural and authentic confidence, instead of a forced portrayal of self-importance.

Of course, we won't be perfect in our execution of living any of our beliefs nor will we be perfect in our ability to hear and follow our work callings. The commitment needed here is to choose to focus on integrating our beliefs into all areas of our lives as the highest priority—and humility is essential in enabling us to do our best work. Humility allows us to be content with who we are, while being called to daring places. We will continue to revisit the belief of humility throughout the book, but now pause and reflect on how living in humility could lead you to greater fulfillment.

CHAPTER 2

SURRENDER

Surrender is our belief in the perfect order of the spiritual world. To believe in surrender is to release any illusion of being able to control the outcomes of our actions. When we surrender, we cease to resist what is happening, which frees us to focus on our experience. Surrender is the only path to embrace joy in our work without worrying about the future.

LEARNING TO LIVE WITH WHAT IS

At work, surrender can appear to be the antithesis of success. We are told to fight, not surrender. To fight for new customers and greater market share, for raises, promotions, and more exposure. Wanting and working for more is considered a mark of a motivated leader, yet our spiritual beliefs tell us we should be living in contentment with what is and at peace with whatever happens. Once again, it seems that our spiritual beliefs have to exist separately from the demands of our work lives.

My job provides a front-row seat to the dilemmas faced by executives trying to integrate surrender into their professional careers. It is also a topic that came up in discussion recently with one of my clients. She was preparing to move her family across the country for a new job. As we talked, she mentioned how she'd shared with her previous leadership team her belief that striving for goals was the essence of a fulfilled life. In her view, people thrived when in pursuit of something. The most senior person at the table disagreed. He felt that cultivating contentment was the only path to true fulfillment. She was perplexed by how a senior leader could hold those views and wondered what it would have meant for her career growth to work under a leader that wasn't constantly motivated to achieve more.

As she shared the story with me, I was struck by how much I agreed with both positions. Yet, I found it difficult to align the two ideas with each other. I believed that the pursuit of meaningful goals was a component of a fulfilled life *and* I believed that being content with the present situation was important as well. Could both be true?

It can seem as if striving in our work lives and contentment in our spiritual lives are perpetually at odds with each other. Striving is key in reaching any goal. It drives us to seek challenge and growth. How can that be a bad thing?

My client wasn't someone who strived simply for the sake of external gains. She was passionate about her work's mission. Her work helped get life-saving therapies developed and delivered to patients. She also practiced self-sacrifice in her own career when her goals had an adverse impact on the people she loved. She wasn't striving for money or prestige alone, though she was gaining both in the process. Her striving was rooted in trust that her life might have a greater purpose and that was the source of her motivation. Her striving wasn't at odds with her colleague's view of contentment, but it is for many of us. I know that I learned early on to associate motivation with struggle.

The antonym of the word "surrender" is not "strive" but "resist." For most of my career, I wasn't motivated by a mission or purpose but a desire to resist what was currently happening in my life. When I set a goal, I wasn't content with the pursuit of it. I struggled with it and I resisted my current circumstances in favor of my dreams of what a new and better life could bring. I was striving for more money and focused on not having enough right now. I was striving to change my job because I didn't like the current one.

My goals fueled a constant source of unease and displeasure with my current life. The pursuit didn't feel fulfilling or enjoyable, but anxious and tiring. I tried to anticipate problems and manipulate situations to speed up success whenever I could. I was motivated to work hard for fear that I might fail. I found myself (and still find at times) unable to strive and surrender at the same time. Now I've found that integrating my belief in surrender with my work life has turned out to be a more efficient and effective way of getting what I really want, but also keeps me at peace with what is in my present life.

THE QUESTION: SURRENDERING TO OUR LIFE EXPERIENCE

As we move from belief to belief, we'll explore how each one is part of a spiritual process meant to transform our lives. Showing how our spiritual beliefs work together helps us better understand how to integrate those beliefs with our work. We looked at humility in the previous chapter and living in humility ensures we have the capacity to move on to the next step in our show's creation. A mind grounded in humility has the energy and focus needed to build the life our soul desires.

If humility is where spirituality starts, then surrender is where it ends. Surrendering to God and to life itself is where the spiritual journey is trying to take us. My beliefs called me to surrender my will to God. Yet, I found it difficult to let go of my desire to feel in control. I also struggled to pursue a goal and still be at peace with whatever happened.

Similar to humility, some of the questions that we will explore in this chapter are:

- What do we believe about surrender?
- Why is surrender spiritually important?

- Is surrender relevant to our work lives?
- Do we need surrender to live in fulfillment?

But ultimately, the purpose of this chapter is to guide you to reflect and answer one question:

Q: Is your belief in surrender integrated into your life?

Surrender (like humility) is a belief in taking an action that relieves unnecessary mental distractions and so redirects how we use our time. It is therefore the next step in creating the foundation of our show. So, would you say that this statement is true or false for you?

I believe in a power greater than my individual will. I believe that I cannot anticipate nor control what will happen in my life and I am most fulfilled when I can accept and embrace the beauty and humor in my life experience.

- Do you believe in a spiritual power that is greater than your individual will?
- Do you believe that much of your life experience is out of your control?
- Do you desire the fulfillment that comes from peace of mind?

If the statement is true about what you believe, then you already see the spiritual benefits of integrating surrender into your life. It brings contentment and peace.

I have struggled with all of the beliefs we will be covering. I continue to work on them daily, but it may be fair to say that surrender is the one that challenges me the most. I know that without surrender, I will worry unnecessarily. I know that without surrender, I will steer my words and actions toward things that are based in fear or control and not toward the things God is calling me to. I also struggle to fully integrate surrender when the stakes in the real world are high. I might think to myself, *I'll surrender if the decision is small, but I'm accountable to my family so I can't go surrendering when money is on the line.* But what I've finally realized is that I had an inflated view of my own ability to impact the circumstances, outsmart the players, and control the outcomes. I had to trust in a spiritual world that would create the show I was meant to be living. What I finally realized (and am still working on) is:

The point of spiritual surrender is to free us to focus on the beautiful experience of our lives instead of the stakes themselves.

THE GENRE

The humble version of your show is about the plight of all living beings. Your character makes a valuable but limited appearance only during your lifespan. The next question is to decide on the genre, as this impacts everything from the show's motivations to the characters' goals. So, when writing your show, surrender asks us to decide whether it is a drama or a comedy.

Dramas are known for the depth of emotions they inspire in their viewers and evoke multiple intense feelings during an episode. Most often these are feelings of anticipation, suspense, fear, exhilaration, and surprise. In a drama, we focus our attention on the plot and try to anticipate what will happen next, what we want to happen, and what we fear will happen.

Comedies on the other hand, are designed to produce only one emotion—amusement. Rather than anticipating the plot, the focus is on how you are experiencing the show. Is it funny? Are you enjoying it?

These two genres have contrasting goals and decide everything from how they are written, acted, and ultimately how viewers feel while watching them. Writers take pride in creating unique stories, but often there is consistency in the structure of the plot regardless of genre. German novelist Gustav Freytag wrote *Die Technik des Dramas*, a study of the five-act dramatic structure, in 1863. The study continues to be widely referenced today for the concept of Freytag's pyramid which outlines the development of plots.

Under Freytag's pyramid, the plot consists of five parts: exposition, rising action, climax, falling action, and dénouement, as is shown in the following illustration:

FREYTAG'S PYRAMID

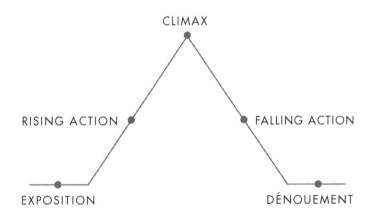

- *Exposition:* The audience is given the backstory, which provides context for the main story and character motivations. Often these are delivered through dialogue, flashbacks, or additional setting details.

- *Rising Action:* A series of events that build increasing interest in the story.

- *Climax:* The highest point of interest when the conflict must be resolved to move the story forward.

- *Falling Action:* The events that address the conflict.

- *Dénouement:* The conflict is either explained or resolved.

The arc is not always sloped the same way, but these elements feature in most storylines. Dramas and comedies may have different goals, but they both use the same elements to set the scene, drive the action to a decision point, and resolve conflicts. Each of these steps also mirror how the conflicts in our lives play out.

- **Exposition:** Our show has its own exposition, which is all of world history, everyone else's backstory and baggage, and this helps us understand the setting in which the conflicts will play out and reveal the motives of the other characters.

- **Rising Action:** This is where we spend the bulk of our lives, as the rising action builds interest and continues our storylines toward points of conflict.

- **Climax:** Those real-life conflicts that must be resolved. Should we break up or stay together? Should I look for a new job? Is he/she a real friend? Will my business be successful? How will I pay my bills?

- **Falling Action:** This is where we engage directly with these issues, making conscious or unconscious decisions that drive our actions.

- **Dénouement:** When we arrive at a final answer and/or the situation is stabilized.

The process occurs over and over again in our lives. Deciding whether or not to live in surrender won't help us avoid it, or eliminate any of the stages, because conflicts are a predictable part of being alive. We will have to make tough decisions and then put those decisions into action.

Deciding whether or not to live in surrender is about *how* we want to view those conflicts and *how* we choose to experience each stage. Do you want your show to be an emotional drama or an amusing comedy? How will that decision impact the way you experience life? Which show genre will lead to greater fulfillment?

Depending on the genre, viewers come to each episode with expectations about what they'll experience. Since dramas and comedies have different motivations, we view their episodes focusing on the information most relevant to that genre.

The conflict in a drama is the main focus. The entire purpose of the episode is to address it or face negative consequences. There is a lot to lose in a drama—your life, your family, your career, your money, your reputation, the love of your life, and sometimes all of those things. The focus of a drama is rooted in fear and a need for triumph and control. Characters must avoid loss and conquer obstacles in a drama. The conflict holds the viewers' attention with great intensity. This is what makes a drama both torturous and surprisingly thrilling to watch. Dramas are captivating, and viewers are drawn into the emotions and anticipation, even if that makes them anxious.

Similarly, if we choose to live in drama, we choose a life where we must learn to successfully control the outcomes of our conflicts. If the genre of your show/life is drama, then you can count on frequently experiencing anxiety, anticipation, suspense, fear, exhilaration, and surprise. Our focus in life will be on our conflicts.

Comedies find common truths in the human condition and then exaggerate those truths to make us laugh. When we watch a comedy, we engage in the conflicts without fear. It is a comedy after all, so how badly could it turn out? Within that safe place, we trust that the conflict will be addressed in a satisfactory way. We then focus our attention more on the characters' interactions than the conflict. As we watch, we relate to the illustration of the characters and laugh at the inherent truth and absurdity of the human condition. Our focus is on the characters' experiences.

If you choose to make your show a comedy, you choose to see life as a series of episodes where you observe the human condition with good humor and acceptance.

PAYING ATTENTION

Often surrender is depicted as *giving up* control, but it is less about what we give up and more about what we *pay attention to*. Surrender, like humility (and discipline, which we'll explore in the next chapter) is integrated into our lives when we purposefully shift our attention and redirect our thoughts. The mind living in a drama will spend each stage of the dramatic arc building tension and stronger emotions. The mind living in a drama focuses on what it has to manipulate and what it has to lose. The stakes are always high in a drama.

When our minds are focused on living in surrender, we redirect our attention to the characters around us and the humor in life. The mind will still see the need to get through conflicts, but it will approach them with curiosity. Instead of fearing the conflict, our thoughts will be redirected toward observations of the experience.

Which show would you rather live in?

EXERCISE

For the next few days, start becoming accustomed to perceiving conflicts rather than getting caught up in them. Conflicts are situations or experiences that trigger you to get stressed or feel emotional and can be due to anything from dealing with a difficult teen in the morning to coping with the evening traffic or a boss demanding that you meet a tough deadline. When you spot conflict, pause and take a breath. Then, instead of trying to fix it or pick the correct answer, ask yourself questions like:

· What does this experience feel like for me and any others involved?

· What have others done in similar circumstances and how did it turn out?

· What am I learning from this?

> • Are there any parts of this experience that are interesting or amusing?
>
> By watching your episodes unfold with greater detail, and looking with interest and amusement even while you are experiencing conflict, you create enough emotional distance between yourself and the conflict to enjoy and observe the journey.

YOUR CHOICE:
TO RELEASE YOUR FEARS

Beliefs that don't transform the way we live are meaningless. We seek out beliefs usually due to a desire to shift from fear-based suffering to purpose-based living. Our belief in humility provides a solution to our fear of insignificance. Surrender provides a solution to our fear of being helpless.

EXERCISE

As you work to answer the main question of this chapter *(Is your belief in surrender integrated into your life?)*, take your journal and consider whether fear is playing a major role in your experience.

• Would you describe your life experience as peaceful and content?

> • Is fear factoring into most of the thoughts that pass through your mind during the day?
> • Is fear driving your decisions?

Each of us are at different places on the spectrum of surrender; it is not an all-or-nothing task to live in surrender. But take time to think about where you fall on that spectrum and how that impacts your work. If you are already doing fairly well with integrating surrender, commit to staying in that place.

Fear is a powerful driver in the mind, which is why we need to release our fears before we can be proactive about our life decisions. Letting surrender redirect our focus to the human experience demotes fear's role from being the primary driver of our life. It is a critical step in building the beautiful life experience we desire—one that is flowing with possibility while we enjoy the ride.

Our beliefs are not a goal to be achieved and then put on a shelf like a trophy. Every day we have to renew our commitment to what we believe by the way we live our lives.

Fears have a way of driving not just our major decisions, but also our smaller decisions and our habits too. In this way, fear can create our life. When we choose to surrender, we don't actually give up control. We never had control in the first place. We simply give up the illusion of it.

Unexpected and uncontrollable change is inevitable. Complete control over the storylines of our lives is not possible—no matter how hard we try. It is inevitable that, at one time or another, we will be separated from our loved ones. Our health will fail eventually. Our youth will fade. Our jobs will end. Our finances will fluctuate. All of these changes are unavoidable and even predictable. Fear does not stop them from coming.

The same is true for the positive changes in life too. New loved ones will enter our lives—through birth or life experience. Wisdom and growth will come. Some relationships will flourish and deepen. New jobs will start. We will get up day after day with yet another new opportunity to experience the miracle of life. Then one day, we will no longer have an opportunity to do so and our lives will be over. Surrender makes sure we made the most of our time here. Surrender makes sure we stay connected enough to God to appreciate the gift of experiencing the life that was given to us.

What we ultimately want from our beliefs is a path to live our practical lives integrated with our spiritual lives. Surrender makes room for that to be possible. Surrender changes the motivation of your show from a place where you must conquer to survive to a place where you observe, experience, and laugh (as often as you can). In the show with surrender, our capacity to focus on our work is magnified. Fear doesn't stop us from pursuing the things we really want because we can live with the outcome either way. It is only through surrender that we are able to strive and be content at the same time.

Our souls are here to embrace and experience our lives as a miraculous gift. Humility and surrender focus us enough so that we can strive for the goals our soul calls us to (more on this later) instead of the ones that are rooted in real-world, or material, thinking. Bringing surrender to our work frees us to peel away our layers of protection and the masks of achievement to reveal who we are. The thing we all want most from our work is to have it be a meaningful expression of our truest (and therefore spiritual) selves.

Before we move on, take another moment to reflect on surrender and how it could lead you to greater fulfillment.

When surrender turns down the dial on your fears, it turns up your ability to let your authentic self show up in the world.

CHAPTER 3

DISCIPLINE

Discipline is a belief in the unlimited human potential to grow and evolve. Being disciplined means we have the ability to align our habits in the human world with what our soul desires. While many people associate discipline with rigidity, it is more closely correlated with the flexibility to change. Discipline allows us to find, follow, and grow into future work callings that are beyond our present capabilities.

WHO DO YOU WANT TO BE?

The most common question asked of children is, "What do you want to be when you grow up?" Life seems to encourage us to focus on work and pick a path as soon as possible. For some, following a career starts while they are still teenagers—choosing which classes to take and clubs or programs to shape their trajectory into future academic pursuits or employment.

Choosing a career is the hardest of all work decisions because it is difficult to know if we are making the right choice. Will we later regret this decision? Will we waste time or money pursuing work we ultimately won't enjoy? It is impossible to choose one career path without moving further away from another. So, in the pursuit of success, most of us try to follow a predetermined plan to check the boxes of credentials, achievements, and experiences relevant to our chosen field. We work to build a career story that will tell the world who we are.

A resume (or CV) is the summary of that story and recruiters use it to assess whether you are a close enough match to their position to warrant an interview. Meeting the minimum requirements alone won't get you the job, but it will tell the recruiter that you are worth moving to the next stage. Your resume looks back at what you have done to date and makes a case for who you are currently and what you would likely bring to the job.

Recruiters prefer a resume that tells a consistent story, one that shows that you have done similar things with increasing scope or scale for long enough to have expertise. A good resume has lengthy tenures of employment that suggest you will stay at a new employer longer. Resumes are helpful in predicting what you might do, based on your previous patterns. And while previous patterns are certainly important data points, they assume that a candidate will remain the same.

Where the best recruiters prove their value is in being able to assess who someone currently is, but also predict their potential to grow. Those recruiters can explain to a hiring manager why a candidate fits the needs of the current opening, but also why they have potential to become an even more valuable contributor in the future.

THE QUESTION:
THE DISCIPLINE TO EMBRACE CHANGE

Our spiritual belief in discipline shifts our focus from who we have been to who we can become. Spiritual discipline is about having the dexterity to set our old self aside (without shame, regret, or limits) so we can embrace the process of change. For this reason, the next belief statement is a bit more complex than the last two. You may want to read it a few times or pause after reading it before deciding if the statement is true for you.

I believe that I am a spiritual being capable of growing and changing. My identity is flexible and not permanently shaped by my past actions. I am most fulfilled when I can use discipline to build habits that reflect the desires of my soul.

This leads us to the question for this chapter:

Q: Have you integrated your belief in discipline into your life?

I used to think of discipline as having the strength to make myself do what was good for me. Yet often these were the things I struggled the most to do or didn't even want to do. I simply thought I *should* be doing them. Some of the real-life reasons I have tried to summon the power of discipline over the years are:

- To start, restart, or show greater consistency when working on a passion project.

- To increase how often I read for knowledge or self-development.

- To increase how often I made healthy food choices.

- To start working out again or increase the frequency I was getting it done.

- To increase how often I gave loved ones my undivided attention.

- To increase how often I practiced my spiritual rituals—be that attending services consistently, praying more, or dedicating the time to meditate.

Discipline was a belief I was unable to integrate into my life. I would start out strong, but my resolve would fizzle out before making any sustainable habits. I felt as if I was in battle with myself. There was a fight happening between the person I was and the person I wanted to be. But thinking I knew who "I was" was exactly what made the integration process impossible. I self-sabotaged by doubting my ability to change. I was tied to a rigid view of who I was in the past and not open to the potential of who I could be.

I could plan out an entire career in one setting for the person that is going to stay mostly the same

There is safety in the idea that we know who we are and what we are capable of. Life is more predictable, if we know who we will continue to be in the future.

throughout their life. If skills, strengths, and passions were fixed, we could create a plan and feel secure in following it. But if we are going to keep changing then we have to be prepared to create new plans that match who we become. Letting go of the fixed identity we have for ourselves means letting in unpredictability about what the future might entail.

Humility, surrender, and discipline are decisions that first ask what we are willing to let go of to gain the spiritual fulfillment we are seeking. To live in humility, we have to ask ourselves whether we are willing to let go of the feeling of being "special." To live in surrender the question is whether we are willing to let go of the feeling of being "in control." With discipline, the question is whether we are willing to let go of the security that we know who we are.

Letting go of our identification with our attributes, and even our problems, is harder than you might think. To this day, I cannot understand why I held on to my connection with "human Kourtney" (as opposed to my more authentic soul) for so long when she was (and still is) quite limited and problematic. I wanted to live in the unlimited fullness of my spiritual self without having to release my rigid identification with my fixed human self. Human Kourtney had become someone I knew well and even with all her issues that familiarity was a comfort to me.

This left me feeling pulled in opposite directions. I wanted to become closer to my spiritual self and use discipline to change the way I was living, but my thoughts and actions didn't reflect that. I was under the mistaken idea that a lack of discipline was my problem. I thought it was a part of my personality that I would always lack. Instead discipline was a spiritual belief that I had to learn how to practice.

EXERCISE

Take out your journal and write down your answers to the following questions:

- Do you know who you are? Are you skeptical about whether you can change?
- What traits do you identify with as being fixed and permanent parts of your personality?
- Are you willing to let go of the comfort and familiarity you have with your identity?
- Are you willing to let yourself become someone that might be quite different from who you are today?

Each of our beliefs requires us to shift where we place our attention and how we direct our thoughts. To live in discipline, our minds have to shift from thinking *we know who we are* to be flexible enough to discover *who God would have us to be.*

We cannot live a life with our souls or higher selves (whichever concept you prefer) in charge, until we are ready to demote our human sense of self. My soul is capable of integrating all the beliefs that will come in future chapters through every part of my life. My soul is grateful, connected, loving, powerful, and patient already. Yet, I couldn't even begin to manifest those beliefs into my real world until I started releasing deep-rooted attachment to my ego-driven human identity. I couldn't use discipline to grow and change, nor birth the work I was called to, when I wasn't *willing* to let my soul fully emerge and be the director of my life choices.

THE FORMAT

Our beliefs build a show that is about all of humanity with us as a valid (but not main) character, and it's a comedy that observes the often-amusing human experience. The next decisions related to discipline are:

- How do we want to experience the episodes of our life?

- Which format of delivery will align with our spiritual beliefs?

Our beliefs work together to help us make decisions. When deciding to live in surrender and make your show a comedy, your choices for format are limited. A comedy wouldn't make a documentary, as that requires realism and its main purpose is to inform. Neither would a comedy work as a TV movie or mini-series, as these are reserved almost exclusively for dramas where the conflict can be highlighted with greater intensity over a short period of time. So, since your show is a comedy the production question for discipline is whether it should be formatted as a variety show or a sitcom.

A variety show delivers humor via sketches. As the title suggests, each sketch is different from the next and the episodes give the viewer a variety of experiences. Freytag's pyramid, which we explored in detail in Chapter 2, is generally used multiple times to quickly illustrate several storylines per episode. Variety shows are often longer in length than a sitcom to allow time for the multiple sketches. There may also be special segments such as musical guests.

Variety shows frequently draw upon current events for their setting and emphasize satire over character development. Each sketch is so short that the focus is placed on making sure the character being portrayed is recognizable (as either a celebrity, political figure, or stereotype). Variety shows differ from sitcoms in that they don't have set, recurring characters though some characters and scenarios may be repeated based on popularity.

The focus is humorously depicting the characters, rather than the evolution of their traits or life experiences. Therefore, character traits usually remain the same if they reappear in future episodes. Unlike most TV formats, variety shows are written to stand alone from episode to episode. If a variety show ends abruptly, you may miss the show but there wouldn't be any unresolved plot or character questions.

A sitcom features the same characters placed in humorous life situations. Sitcoms provide an often-exaggerated view of the lives of their characters. Freytag's pyramid is generally used only once per episode to illustrate a storyline. The plots are frequently based on the character's everyday life versus current events. Humor is generated by the ongoing development of the character's personality and life circumstances.

Series' storylines run from season to season with the hope of keeping the show on as long as possible. A character's storyline isn't fully formed at the beginning of the show—as in many other formats. The writers have a clear idea of who the characters are in the first season, but they don't know who the characters will become. They simply continue writing from season to season with evolving character development. Since the most successful shows can run for many years, characters remain recognizable if played by the same actor but some of the early prominent traits and key life circumstances may have softened or changed entirely. For example, perhaps the single ladies' man is now happily married or the painfully shy girl from the first season is now fully capable of functioning in social settings.

Choosing to make your show a sitcom versus a variety show means choosing between a life where your character is clearly defined or a life where your character is expected to evolve and change.

RECOGNIZING OURSELVES

Choosing the variety show puts our focus on recognizing the characters, even if that means they can't change and grow. In real life, we choose the desire to recognize ourselves and *know who we are* over allowing ourselves the flexibility to be who we are called to be.

Who we think we are is largely influenced by what we see ourselves doing repeatedly. Our identity is shaped by a series of behaviors that signal messages about who we are. We are constantly affirming or adding to our perception of ourselves. Imagine that you are a gigantic magnet pulling titles and perceived characteristics toward you from your surroundings. It is the outside world that we look to for many of our cues on our identity.

If you notice that you run twice a week, then your magnet will pull in the characteristic of "I'm someone who runs." You then add "being a runner" to your view of yourself. If you notice that you eat junk food every other day, then your magnet will pull in the idea that "I'm someone who eats junk food." This works similarly with the roles we add to our identity. If you notice that you take care of or worry about the well-being of your baby (or child, or teenager or adult child) frequently, then your magnet pulls in the title of "parent" to your view of yourself.

> **EXERCISE**
>
> Take a moment to think about and journal all the titles and traits that you have attracted to yourself. Capturing them all would take a long time but spend a few minutes and see how many you can come up with. What are your titles and what are your traits? Your list will reveal what your magnet is pulling—at least right now, anyway.
>
> Hopefully, your list includes many things that you are happy to be associated with, but I'm sure there will also be a few things that you may plan to change or wish you could change. But for right now, this is your list. This is who you perceive yourself to be in this moment and time. Now notice how many traits and titles on your list are conditional on your assessment of your current behavior.

Once "a runner" stops running for an extended period of time they become "someone who is not a runner" or "someone who used to be a runner." If someone stops eating junk food and starts eating healthy food for an extended period of time, then they would start thinking of themselves as "someone who eats healthy food."

Titles can fluctuate as well. You may hold your title of "daughter" for as long as you and your parents are living, but that title is conditional on their lives. You, however, will exist even if that role went away. The same is true for almost all of our titles—wife, husband, parent, sister, brother, friend, employee, volunteer, CEO, doctor, lawyer, etc. They are based on our current circumstances.

Almost everything we think we know about ourselves is flexible and subject to change.

CHANGE BRINGS FEAR

Change also brings up fear, so instead of facing that fear, we may create the perception of a permanent personality or permanent roles. We do this by repeating the same habits that continuously reaffirm our image of who we were and therefore who we still are. Repetition gives us the illusion that we remain the same. It is not that we stay the same, but that we continuously choose to create a similar version of ourselves. I am not permanently "someone who loves chocolate," I am someone who decides I love chocolate over and over and over again.

Understanding this process is important because we have a creative role to play every time we choose our actions. We always have the power to choose differently and start new cycles. Yet, we often fail to believe we can because we have a permanent sense of "who we are," and this predetermines our actions—when really it is our actions that create the perception of who we think we are. The problem in thinking our identity is predetermined is that "who we think we are, right now" may be so entrenched in our minds that it forms an unconscious pattern that inhibits our ability to change.

If a fixed identity has been your reality, discipline has been an uphill battle. When you let go of the confidence that you "know who you are," you'll be able to view yourself more like a piece of clay that can be molded through every new thought and new behavior.

It is not that we are unable to practice discipline to change or grow. It is that we do not believe we are capable of changing in the first place.

Choosing the sitcom over the variety show is a choice to live in discipline without being afraid of losing your character's identity. Discipline threatens our ability to seek comfort in our old self. We have to be willing to part with the feeling that we know ourselves to make room for who we can become.

It is through habits that you shape your character. When you choose to live in discipline, you acknowledge that your character is not defined by your past. You acknowledge that your soul is more important than the world may currently perceive and that gives you the power to use the process of discipline to grow without the pressure of making discipline an "all-or-nothing" personality trait.

The format written with discipline creates a sitcom, because even though your character may be clear in the current episode or season, who they will be in the future remains unwritten.

YOUR CHOICE:
TO FREE YOURSELF

Discipline used to be a word I avoided, as it reminded me that I *wasn't* good enough. It is now one of my favorite words because it is tied to the creative power of God. Discipline is meant to free us more than restrict us; it reminds us that we can connect to our soul and start writing a different story for ourselves whenever we want.

Discipline empowers us to take accountability for the spiritual and human life we are living. A person that integrates discipline knows that they have the power to make new decisions that shape their episodes. They know that living in discipline means not being afraid to be someone else and to go places they never imagined. Take a moment to consider: Are you willing to let yourself become someone else?

For so long I was sure I knew "who I was" and that person *wasn't* so bad. I had my good days. But that person harbored many self-defeating thoughts about what I was capable of. Some of the thoughts that impacted my work the most were:

- **I am** someone who starts things but doesn't finish them.

- **I am** an all-or-nothing kind of person. I cannot live in moderation.

- **I am** someone who has never been consistent enough to be disciplined.

- **I am** unmotivated. I guess I just do not want things badly enough to stay focused and follow through completely.

As I look at the above list now, it is obvious how these beliefs impacted my ability to manifest what God was calling me to. I gave up or doubted myself instead of trusting God to see me through. It was a cycle I had to release so that I could hear my work callings and then start to follow them.

Do you have thoughts about who you are that you have to release to live the next season of your life? Who is your character becoming? By integrating discipline into your life, you have an opportunity to be who *you need to be*, and also release who you thought *you could not be*. I had to learn that discipline is not about willpower, but about flexibility and growth.

There is no need to beat yourself up when you don't follow through on every new resolution or habit.

Instead spend more time observing the thoughts and circumstances that led you there.

Discipline is about getting your mind and your actions working together and taking it one step at a time.

Your show is a comedy so don't forget to relax and enjoy the experience. Laugh at the failures. But also know that as long as your show is running and you're working to put your soul in charge, you will eventually break negative cycles and evolve. All that discipline requires of you is to believe you have the power to do so.

We are not our resumes and God is not judging us based solely on our past. We are human souls here to experience the fullness of our lives. That process will be long, and it will have many twists and turns. Choosing to live in discipline gives us the ability to follow the journey wherever it leads.

THE STORY SO FAR...

Before we move on to the next five beliefs, let's pause for a brief recap on the first three. Humility, surrender, and discipline form the foundation of our spiritual lives. They are therefore a critical piece of learning because they work together to transform who we think we are and what we think we are capable of. The latter has a huge impact on the work we can and will pursue.

All three beliefs seek to create room for our higher self (or soul) to emerge and take the reins of our everyday life. This is the point of having a spiritual practice in the first place. We seek one out to release the worries of the world in exchange for the joy and fulfillment that comes from letting our soul rise to the surface and living in the present moment.

Think about the implications these beliefs have already had on our TV show metaphor. By integrating just these three beliefs, we have created a vastly different show than the one our human impulses might lead us to. We have also previewed how these beliefs will impact us in our work lives though we get into that much more in Part II.

The next five beliefs are less about how we view and connect with our souls and more about how we engage with the world around us. The next five beliefs will write our daily episodes. But before you move on to the next chapter, I encourage you to spend some time in whatever spiritual practice you gravitate toward and pray, meditate, or reflect on the transformative power of humility, surrender, and discipline. Think about how you answered each question. Consider how you want to grow into, or further integrate, those beliefs into your life.

- Are you living in the show you want to be creating?
- Are you able to see yourself as truly equal to those with all the talents, riches, and power in the world?
- Are you able to see yourself as equal to those that are struggling greatly?
- Is life mostly a joyful and amusing experience?
- Is your character free to change and grow above and beyond any fixed views you may have about your identity?
- Think about and name any negative beliefs you may harbor about "who you are" that you need to release.

Doing this work can help you understand how your beliefs can work together to manifest your highest work, but it is only a mental framework. It is meant to speak to your mind. You have to translate it to your heart.

CHAPTER 4

GRATITUDE

Gratitude is our belief in the miraculous and inexplicable gifts present in every life. We practice gratitude by directing and redirecting our attention toward the abundance of life's blessings. No matter what is going on in our home or work lives, most of us can find something to be grateful for—the miracle of water flowing from the faucet, our morning coffee, our friends and family, and so on. Our highest work emerges from gratitude because it focuses us to see the miracle of life that surrounds us in the human experience and can help us find purpose and meaning.

SHAPING OUR STORY

There are some basic tips I give everyone when preparing for a job interview. Be on time. Research the company. Know your resume. Be sure to listen closely and make a personal connection to the interviewer. All of these things are important, but once you nail these, there is another level of interview preparation that is less about *what* you do and more about *how* you do it.

Those that interview well are skilled in telling the story of their career, rather than simply reciting the details. When I coach someone for an interview, we don't focus on the correct answers, but on deciding on the story of "who they are"—what we want the interviewer to take away from the meeting. We then work to draw attention to that story with each answer given. And the most effective way to do this is with the use of examples. My clients prepare a few examples that they could share, if appropriate, during the course of the interview. Often these examples are queued up when asked a skill or behavioral question, such as, *do you have experience in x?* Or *tell me about a time when you had to y?*

It is important to answer interview questions fully and completely with facts and details, but by telling the interviewer a specific example, you have the opportunity to not only provide clarity on your experience but also reinforce the story you want to project. Ideally, you want to tell them more about yourself than what they can deduce simply from looking at the jobs on your resume.

I work with clients to structure the way they tell their examples to make sure they give context that reinforces their themes and orients the interviewer's perspective. If you want to be seen as a "strategic thinker," you'll need to illustrate it by the details you choose to focus on and the ones you choose to omit. For example, you may be asked a question about a time you launched a new product. If you want to show that you are a strategic thinker, then you want to focus the interviewer's attention on your ability to link your actions to the overall strategy. You want to start your example by explaining what was occurring in the industry, then what was happening at your company in particular. It is only after you share those big picture details that you would then be able to describe the specific product launch's role in meeting your company's strategy. At the end of the example, you'd finish the story by telling them the impact your launch had on realizing the company goals.

The interviewer then leaves your discussion not only understanding your product launch skills (which was the question they asked you), but also seeing you as someone that is oriented toward aligning strategy to make a tangible impact. They don't form the opinion that you are a strategic thinker because you told them so. They form the opinion because they think they had their own flash of insight into who you are. And they are more likely to remember what they thought about you and why because stories tend to be more memorable than listing details.

If you only recite a summary of your product launch experience, you would miss the opportunity of giving the interviewer more context and shaping their perspective about the unique value you would bring. In a similar way to interview technique, gratitude shapes the story of our spiritual life, because it draws our attention to examples

Within gratitude lies the ability to change our perspective and therefore change how we are experiencing our lives.

of the value of our life experience. Gratitude gives context and perspective by focusing our attention on who we are in the spiritual world and all the blessings that abound because of it.

THE QUESTION: GRATITUDE FOR EVERYTHING

Few would argue against the benefits of living in gratitude and many studies have proved its value to our health (mentally, physically, and spiritually). Many of us have chosen to start gratitude journals in an effort to focus more on our daily blessings. This ritual is meant to remind us of the many things we have been given.

Being thankful for what we have is the first step in the path to living in gratitude. The next step is learning how to place our attention on the absence of things we don't have to endure. This presents our greatest opportunity for grateful living but, similar to our career story, keeping our focus on this kind of gratitude requires preparation and effort.

Going into an interview and simply answering questions is easy. Having a story ready that will draw their attention to a specific theme requires preparation. Doing the work to bring greater awareness to our vast blessings is what it means to live in gratitude. So, this chapter is asking you to reflect on your daily thoughts and decide:

Q: Have I integrated what I believe about gratitude into my life?

Is this belief statement true or false for you?

I believe that my life is a divine gift and there are always things I can be thankful for. I am most fulfilled when I do the work to focus my attention on my blessings.

Context and perspective help us to see the bigger picture and orient the story we tell ourselves about what is happening. When we understand something in context it shapes our perspective. For example, look at the following quote:

> In my mind I took bus rides, unlocked the front door of my apartment, answered my telephone, switched on the electric lights.

It seems like a simple sentence with several mundane, even trivial, actions. That is until you realize it was written by Viktor Frankl to describe his longings while in a Nazi concentration camp. Does that additional information give the sentence a different meaning for you? If so, that is the power of context. It makes us feel differently about the same information. Now let's read it with the next line included.

> In my mind I took bus rides, unlocked the front door of my apartment, answered my telephone, switched on the electric lights. Our thoughts often centered on such details, and these memories could move one to tears.

With even more information, we see that these actions from Viktor's perspective were luxuries. They were huge blessings; they were things that he deeply longed for. Likely, these are all luxuries that you have in your life presently, and you do many of these things right now.

Focusing on Viktor's story takes us beyond reading his words. It helps us understand the deeper meaning of what Viktor was expressing. Gratitude is taking that perspective and viewing your own experiences differently be-

The most joyful among us are those that actively work to see their blessings in greater context and let it shape the perspective on the story of their life.

cause of it. Gratitude is noticing when you switch on the lights and pausing to think about what a blessing that is. Viktor once longed to do that same action, and someone somewhere is still longing for it.

THE BACKSTORY

The first three beliefs—humility, surrender, and discipline—address how we engage with our spiritual selves. Gratitude is the first of five beliefs that orients how we engage daily with the human world.

Until now, we have been playing the role of the producer and deciding what kind of show we want to live. Now it is time for the writers to get to work to craft each episode: the settings, character motivations, and all the words and actions. The producer has made some decisions on the type of show, but the writers are going to create the show one episode at a time.

Remember Freytag's pyramid in Chapter 2 and how the plot consists of five parts: exposition, rising action, climax, falling action, and dénouement? Now you have to make some decisions about what you want your character's role to be in each phase of the arc. Choosing gratitude is tied to the exposition stage.

Exposition gives the audience context on where you are in the story, who is there with you, and provides any relevant backstory for the various characters. The writers don't have to know exactly what the characters will say or do, or even how the conflicts will be resolved, but they do need to know what the climax of an episode is supposed to be in order to write the appropriate context into the exposition. Otherwise, they run the risk of focusing on more details than are relevant or omitting details that are critical to understanding the characters' perspective.

We won't be exploring your show's climax until Chapter 6 but keep in the back of your mind that it is when we explore the belief of love. If we want to be living in a show that is anchored by our spiritual beliefs, then our lives are meant to climax with love and our exposition written with gratitude is meant to start us on that journey.

Several key pieces of the storyline are set into motion by the exposition:

- Timeframe

- Location

- Relevant historical events

- Character history

- Character motivation

Humility, surrender, and discipline have empowered us to create a sitcom about humanity. Thankfully, the producer has chosen to focus on the routine aspects of life—evaluating a new love interest, throwing a party, getting a new job, etc. In the exposition, our writers have to make decisions to give the audience the appropriate context or the episode could go astray. The decision about choosing to live in gratitude is the same. As we approach each new day/episode we are asked to set the context and perspective for our storyline. We are asked to repeatedly answer the questions:

- Where do I fit in the timeline of my story?

- Where is my story taking place?

- Who are the characters in my story?

Choosing to live in gratitude will dramatically change the way you view the answers to these questions, and it will shape the foundation of your storyline. We all have things that are blessings for us, but not for others. Our ability to see those things is critical to fully experiencing gratitude. In order to do that, we need to seek out the knowledge that puts our lives in context. We have to work to get information that is not obvious at first glance.

EXERCISE

Take a moment right now and look at whichever is your dominant hand. Pause and take a good look at it. Is the skin smooth or scarred? Are all your fingers fully formed? Is it missing any significant functionality? Is your hand in pain right now?

Try to place your pain level in your hand on a scale of one to ten, where one means you have no pain at all and ten represents the kind of excruciating pain that would make you want to have your hand amputated. How much pain is your hand feeling in this moment?

Whatever number you decided on (for me it is a one) slowly consider what the next number might feel like. What is a two or a three? Continue until you have to imagine having level ten pain.

Many people are born without the full use of their dominant hand. Whatever you use your dominant hand to do today, they cannot experience the same ease of use that you have.

Whatever number you placed your own pain level, there is someone that sits at every single pain number from where you are today right up to a ten. Someone is having their hand amputated right now as you read this.

Your hand's functionality, your hand's relative lack of pain, and your ability to read, instead of preparing for an operation, are all privileges. They are blessings whether we normally notice them or not.

COUNTING YOUR BLESSINGS

Gratitude exercises focus on the enormity of our blessings. It is one thing to write, "I am grateful for my health" to your list of positive things you notice, but another to put the privilege of good health in the context of the human experience. If you are healthy and/or pain free right now, you have an extraordinary gift. There are countless single blessings inherent in all the systems that are working properly for you and all the privileges that that provides. Good health is rarer than you might recognize. If you happen to have it right now, it is worth focusing on how good health is both precious and temporary. Viewing it in that context magnifies the gratitude you experience.

I realize many of you may be experiencing pain and health issues. The hand exercise may not have reminded you of a blessing, but more of the suffering you endure. In your case, try the exercise with something else. Perhaps use some of Viktor Frankl's desires from his days in the concentration camp. One that stuck with me the most from his experiences was to not be granted the ability to know whether his loved ones were dead or alive.

> **EXERCISE**
>
> If a life without pain is not one of your blessings, pause instead to wonder what the next example might feel like.
>
> Are you able to know which of your loved ones are dead and which ones are alive? How would you feel if you had no way of knowing this information? Take a moment to imagine someone specific that you love deeply.
>
> Imagine that you have no way of reaching them. You have no way of knowing if they are alive. You fear they may be dead, but you cannot be sure. Then remind yourself that you are not in that circumstance at the moment.
>
> You do know if they are alive or dead. You could reach out to them right now.

For Viktor, having this knowledge was a privilege—one he longed for. Living with this exact level of emotional uncertainty and heartache is something many people around the world continue to endure today. They are wondering about loved ones right now. You may have this privilege despite your physical suffering.

That doesn't change or diminish the pain your body may be experiencing, but it can change the context that you view your life's episodes. Magnifying gratitude is the first step for setting the context of our storylines of love.

Often when the word "privilege" is used it is applied to the privileges granted to certain groups by racial, religious, sexual orientation, or socioeconomic factors. We will not be limiting the use of the word to only those factors, but those factors are definitely something you should also consider about your life.

Resist the natural inclination to avoid thinking about systematic privileges for fear of feeling guilty or complicit. You didn't design the world, but it is your job to see it clearly if you hope your work will make it better.

Studying history, listening to the pain of others, and following current events can provide you with more than enough context to examine your privileges. You just have to choose to focus on seeking out and letting that information in. You may also like to ask yourself, "Do I have positive things (or lack negative things) in my life due to no effort of my own?" If so, in what ways? Decide to bring your privileges and blessings into full focus so you can show the appropriate gratitude for them. Bring them into focus so you don't risk

Understanding what you have—your blessings and also your privileges—sets the context for your show about humanity.

misinterpreting or misrepresenting the context under which your life stories should be written.

Are you suffering and struggling or are you privileged and blessed? The same life can tell either story. You get to decide what context your writers are going to focus on. We tend to be pretty good at seeing where life has been unkind to us, but seeing privileges requires working to bring them into view. Despite our real hardships, there are still many circumstances where each of us are abundantly blessed.

Start wondering why you have been so blessed because genuine curiosity for that question is required to start the process of finding your work callings.

YOUR CHOICE: TO SEE ABUNDANT BLESSINGS

When we let in the disadvantages and pain of others, we experience gratitude on a whole new level. Just for today, try to seek out more information about the human experience. Deeply consider how your life compares— sometimes you will see privileges in comparison but not always. Choose to focus on the places where you can see blessings. Gratitude will set the perspective of the life and career stories you are about to write.

But gratitude isn't just about seeing only the good but also about the broader context and realizing the good we have within it. Living in gratitude is a decision to set the context of your life around stories of your blessings. This is vital because it's all too easy to lose sight of the context and stories we tell ourselves and they ultimately shape the lives we end up living. The same spouse can be a loving irreplaceable supporter or a selfish disconnected roommate. A lot (not all) of what determines the fate of a long-term relationship is the stories we tell ourselves and reinforce about who our spouse or partner is.

Similarly, in our work lives, we are tasked with deciding who our boss is or what value this current job has. As we head into work every day, we tell ourselves stories of some kind. The purpose of living in gratitude is to decide what you want that story to be. The same difficult job can be an important and temporary learning opportunity that provides a salary that is a fiefdom in some parts of the world, or it can be a torturous and boring waste of your talents. We can get up every day and decide which story we want to tell. We set the context for our episodes by where we place our focus.

Do you realize how amazing it is to have the physical and mental capabilities to perform your job today? Do you realize what a blessing your job is, despite its flaws?

Gratitude comes after humility, surrender, and discipline because we need to have integrated those beliefs before we can create and latch on to these kinds of stories. And if the idea of shifting your work stories to gratitude feels impossible then consider going back to the first three chapters. You are stuck in a show that has yet to be integrated with humility, surrender, and discipline. Humility will both empower you to move past negative mental chatter and build compassion. Surrender will help you release fear and hostile emotions. Discipline will leave you flexible and even excited for the possibilities of who you might become, and where your stories may develop in the future. All three will open the door to the possibility of a new perspective to see stories told in gratitude.

Gratitude has the power to ground the stories of our life and get our episodes moving toward the direction of love.

Perception is reality. Who an interviewer "thinks we are" is all that matters when applying for a job. If it's a positive perception, we receive an offer, if not we don't. More often than not, who our bosses or clients think we are has a greater impact on our success than actual performance. If our perception of our lives is steeped in gratitude, the reality of our lives will take shape differently. We will be attracting and receiving the life that aligns with our perception. We will be living whatever story we choose to tell ourselves.

CHAPTER 5

CONNECTION

Connection is a belief in the interdependence of your life with all other living beings. When living in connection, we actively seek to understand the life experiences of others and bring the kindness and compassion that we seek ourselves from the world, to the world. Practicing connection leads us to new experiences, but also expands and fills our hearts. Connection prepares us to work from a place of wholeness.

TUNING INTO OTHERS

Returning to the topic of interview preparation, there is one tip I hammer home again and again: try to get the interviewer to speak as much as possible. That might seem to be counterintuitive, as most of our preparation focuses on the story we want to tell about ourselves, and the skills and experiences we want to convey. Yet, this tip is by far the most important rule of interviewing in my opinion.

When the interviewer speaks a lot, two things happen. First, they tend to give you the answer to the test about what would make you the best candidate for the job. If you can get the interviewer talking about their vision for the organization and what this role needs, you will know how to shape your responses to their questions. You will know what they really care about and it will help you decide which examples to share and how to frame your experiences.

But second, and perhaps more importantly, when the interviewer speaks an equal amount (if not more) they leave the interview feeling respected and understood. That subconscious feeling makes them view you as a candidate more favorably, even if they actually learned less about your experience. You are more likely to get the job when the interviewer feels understood by you than when you feel most understood by them.

Surprisingly, this tip is something I have to revisit again and again with every interview round. Clients intellectually understand why this tip will work, but in the actual interview setting they struggle to implement it. Once asked a question, their natural desire to be understood takes over and leads to long rambling answers that use up most of the allotted time. They start to worry that they will miss their opportunity to be understood and leave the interview without making the kind of connection that would have been possible if their focus was on the interviewer instead of themselves.

THE QUESTION:
CONNECTING TO OTHERS

A spiritual belief in connection manifests similarly to the above interview tip. Connection is only possible when we are able to shift our viewpoint from a desire to be understood to a desire to understand others. Easier said than done, right?

Again, this is where all the other beliefs come in handy. Once we integrate humility, surrender, discipline, and gratitude, we will have the emotional space to focus on connecting with others. It is hard to shift the focus off ourselves and our real and natural need to be understood, when we are distracted, afraid, or focused on our suffering.

When we are aware of the connection we have to all souls, engaged in the amusing experience of our lives, flexible to who we might become and focused on our blessings, we are primed and ready to connect deeply with others.

We are ready to integrate a spiritual belief in connection into our daily lives. As you read this chapter, prepare to reflect on and answer one main question:

CONNECTION

Q: Have I integrated what I believe about connection into my life?

So, what do you believe about living in connection? Is the next belief statement true or false for you?

I believe that all living beings are connected, and I am fulfilled when I can live in awe and appreciation of the gift of life. I am here to seek to understand others and express the same kindness and compassion I want for myself.

Connection implies that two or more things are tied together. You couldn't harm the ocean without it impacting the waves, and you couldn't harm just a single wave without harming the ocean. The waves and ocean are permanently connected to each other. Do you believe that all living beings are similarly connected?

EXERCISE

Sit quietly for a few moments and imagine discovering that you had an identical twin. For fun, choose a name for your twin. Imagine his or her face looking just like yours with perhaps a different hairstyle and another style of clothing.

Your twin was adopted at birth and raised on another continent. Your lives have been very different. Yet you and your twin look eerily similar.

Their childhood may have been easier or harder than yours. The country they were raised in may have an entirely different culture from your own. Perhaps they speak a different language.

Yet, your physical resemblance is undeniable. They have similar mannerisms. When they smile, you can see yourself. The pitch of their laughter is so much like your own.

Imagine how you might feel about your twin.

Whenever I imagine meeting my twin in this scenario, I instinctually picture myself reaching out to hold their hands or embracing them. Clearly, we are different people and practically strangers but the idea that they are my twin makes me want to reach for them and pull them close.

Being able to recognize physical similarities creates a connection almost instantaneously. No matter what life your twin lived before your meeting, you know that you would immediately care about them. You would have had different experiences, perhaps come from different places, and would clearly be two separate people, but you would be able to see yourself in them.

We are living the belief of connection when we interact with other living beings with the ability to see our own reflection in them. Think about how different it would be to interact with your twin for the first time versus another stranger. You would be much more likely to appreciate their uniqueness, instead of making quick judgments. In many ways, you would be fascinated by your differences, and be curious and eager to understand them better.

How might you feel, if you learned that your twin had experienced a trauma in life before you met them? As they share their suffering, it might not feel like a trauma that happened to a stranger. Instead it happened to someone you are connected to. It may feel as if the trauma could have easily happened to you instead of them.

Curiosity in people, seeking to understand and appreciating similarities, despite your differences, is how living in connection reveals itself.

Our instinct would be to empathize with our twin. If we couldn't personally relate to their circumstances, we would still be motivated to do the work to understand them better. We would ask them to share their experiences. Perhaps we would also do internet research and talk to others in similar circumstances. But most importantly, we would make the effort to be compassionate to them.

It is natural to feel a connection to those that share our DNA, or have obvious similarities, but we are capable of feeling connection with anyone. We have to choose to listen to them, seek out the context, and do the work to understand their feelings. Integrating our belief in connection hinges on the decision to be curious and compassionate.

Choosing to live in connection changes everything about how we interact with people. When we see ourselves in another, we choose to connect more deeply. We are motivated to do the work to relate to them far beyond our personal experiences. Interacting with other living beings transforms our relationships and experiences—which makes building the episodes that lead to a belief in love the obvious next step.

THE FOCUS: RISING ACTION

Connection changes our goals. It shifts our thinking from a desire to be understood to a desire to understand. Living in connection shows that we value being independent and unique, yet still connected to one another. We are all waves in one beautiful ocean. A belief in connection is also closely tied to humility. Connection challenges us to move past the idea that we are so "special" that we are separate from one another. We are not the main characters. We can live in a show that makes room to focus on the storylines of all the other characters.

In the last chapter, we decided to let gratitude set the stage for the exposition of each episode. Whatever you choose to make your episodes about, they must be grounded in the overall point of the show—observing the human experience. In the last chapter, you gave each episode context by focusing on the information that helps you see your privileges and be grateful for your blessings. Now it's time to move on to rising action—the next stage in writing our storyline, as shown in Freytag's pyramid in Chapter 2.

Rising action is the first time the audience sees the events of the storyline actually taking place, as well as getting a feel for what is happening and understanding how each actor plays a role in moving the storyline along. When you look back at Freytag's pyramid, you will see that rising action moves with an uphill trajectory toward the climax of the story. Therefore, it requires increasing upward movement.

This movement is critical to how your episodes will unfold. Rising action is the point between the background or backstory (exposition) and the conflict that must be resolved (climax). How you approach rising action will determine what your conflicts end up being. Focusing the rising action on connection will help keep your story grounded in the beliefs that we've covered so far.

To do this, each and every action made by your character must have the goal of increasing the audience's understanding and compassion for other living beings. Your rising action will illustrate who the characters are and how they relate to each other. As a writer, you will weave each of the characters' unique journeys to create one unified storyline.

If we hope to live in connection, we have to also be willing to weave the storylines of others into the show.

Let's pretend your episode is about a routine day in August. Within this episode there will be other characters having different experiences that may be impacted by the fact that it is the summer.

For some characters, it is their favorite time of the year. The weather is beautiful, and they get to spend more time outside, and with their children. It is also when they take a long vacation to their chosen destination. Then there are other characters who also look forward to the summertime but can only take a shorter vacation with limited options for their destination due to budget. Next there will be those characters that want to take a vacation but cannot afford one. The children are out of school, so this brings additional childcare expenses. A vacation isn't possible this year but perhaps in future years. Finally, there are those characters who can't even think about taking a vacation and dread the summertime, as providing for their basic needs and paying for childcare puts the family and finances under duress.

Clearly there are many other variations of the characters' stories on this August day that are not addressed here. These examples are only meant to illustrate how our writers will write a story where characters have an increasing pursuit to understand each other better. A person that is living in connection is seeking out those with diverse experiences. A person living in connection is intentionally paying attention to and seeking to understand our differences.

LIVING IN CONNECTION

To live in connection, we have to put ourselves in new and varied environments. We have to read different things, seek out diverse sources of information but, most importantly, we have to open our hearts to being interested in connecting to those that are different from us in the first place. When we are committed to understanding the unique circumstances of others we are able to see ourselves in them. Connection is not about sympathizing with others, but about empathizing.

EXERCISE

Imagine living in someone else's shoes, perhaps someone suffering financial hardship or ill health or loss. In order to do so, you'll have to learn more about those shoes.

- What are they like?
- Where did they come from?
- Where would they support us and where might they hurt our feet?
- Are you working hard to understand and connect more deeply with those around you on a daily basis?

Writing your episodes with connection will mean increasing your understanding of the human experience. Someone living in connection doesn't view the summertime as if it was the "best time of the year" for everyone, even if it is for them. They stop to get to know the point of view of all in the show. They find ways to meet and interact with people having different experiences.

What makes it hard to live in connection is that everyone we routinely interact with may in fact be having a similar experience to our own. This means we have to move beyond our own social circle in order to increase our understanding of others in the show. Moving outside our immediate circle requires commitment and effort to integrate our daily episodes with a belief in connection. Connection is also the start of finding what will motivate us enough to follow a work calling. It is the pursuit of connection that puts us in different places with a broader view of life experiences. The pursuit of connection provides new data that reveals where our unique skills can make a difference in the overall show.

Living in connection is important in our spiritual lives; it keeps our show on course, but connection is also a powerful tool in finding the kind of work that calls us.

YOUR CHOICE:
TO MOVE FROM THEM TO US

Connection requires that we move past the inner circle of "us" and "them" and seek out ways to use our time here on this earth to appreciate life itself. In this way, integrating connection into your life will deepen any and all of your existing relationships, from your closest friends to casual business acquaintances; it will also attract new experiences and give you a broader view on the world. We will never run out of ways to increase our ability to live in greater connection, compassion, and understanding, but a spiritual belief in connection also serves to ignite our passions and develop our perspective within the daily episodes of our lives.

In the same way, if we never look up at the stars we will not be awed by them or appreciate them. But if we devote ourselves to regularly looking up at the sky then we have a much better shot at appreciating the miraculous world in which we live and the work of God. If we take it even further and seek out information about the universe and the sky above, we will quickly find many amazing facts that put the stars into context and increase our perspective on what we are looking at. And ultimately, the more we learn the more we will find questions about the universe still left unanswered by science. Our quest to understand will leave us with more facts unknown and things to further explore. We will find ourselves in a spiritual place. We will find ourselves in awe of God and the gift of life.

Deciding to integrate connection into your life opens you to explore the multifaceted experience of others. Are you attempting to have genuine interactions and let in the information that would help you understand better? Are you more focused on your desire to see the value in another and understand their experience or are you more focused on your own need to be valued and understood?

Connection changes the direction of your storyline from impacting a smaller circle to larger, richer, and more interesting pursuits that will motivate you to get to work. If you fear that you lack motivation to follow through with fulfilling your potential, it is probably because you haven't yet written the storylines that will interest you enough. Your engagement with life to date may be too narrow and hasn't given you the data you need on what things you most want to learn about and address in the world.

As we move closer toward our belief in love, the increasing need to open our hearts and minds beyond our own experience is inevitable.

Every spiritual practice instructs us to embrace the impermanence and fluidity of our identity on this earth. Some use phrases like "die to self" or "transcend the ego." No matter what we call it, this concept is rooted in humility, surrender, and discipline, and requires a shift of importance from our own experience to a universal experience. It requires that we move past our tightly held beliefs in ourselves, as being real and the most important, and opening up to the reality of our spiritual selves as real and most important. We make this journey inside our hearts with the integration of our first three beliefs, but as we get deeper into the five beliefs most visible to the world, we reflect this journey by how we live our lives.

What we say and don't say, what we view and read, where we go, who we go with, how we spend our money, and how we use our talents are the manifestation of what we believe. Choosing to live in connection is the most visible fruit of our spiritual life.

CHAPTER 6

LOVE

Love is a belief that living beings are sacred. Love charges us with a responsibility to honor life by living as the purest and fullest expression of ourselves and supporting others in their attempt to do the same. A work life built around love will point us toward our highest callings and require that we overcome the fears that threaten to hold us back.

THE HIGHEST SPIRITUAL DIRECTIVE

At times, my job is part career coach and part therapist. Despite working with many high-performing and high-achieving people, I find myself needing to help my clients see and own their potential. Sometimes I trust in their ability to successfully grow more than they do themselves. In such cases, I encourage them to interview for stretch assignments, new jobs that are a significant promotion in title or scope, or to take a riskier, more entrepreneurial path. It is easy to know what your resume says you have already accomplished and therefore can do, but it is harder to consider what your potential might be.

Love is frequently thought of as the highest spiritual directive. It requires an ability to honor the sacred gift of life. Any decisions rooted in love will reflect this reverence. If we made our career decisions based on love alone, we would be fearless in our pursuit of authentic work and honoring our potential. The markers of love are an ability to grant to ourselves and others the freedom and grace to fully engage with life and realize our potential to be all that God made us to be. Love is about honoring the magnificent beauty and never-ending potential of our precious life.

The challenge in integrating love into our work lives is that decisions made in love can and will make us feel more vulnerable. It is difficult to respect and honor life without putting ourselves at a perceived disadvantage.

In the last chapter, we answered the question of connection by pointing our actions toward things that would help us build a genuine appreciation for the lives around us. Choosing connection is a critical and necessary step for integrating your beliefs into your work, but love is where "the rubber meets the road." In opening our eyes to understanding and appreciating the potential of life, we are called to fully engage in and honor it. We are called to live in love with ourselves, with others, with nature, and with life itself. This requires that we orient our real-world decision-making toward choices that reflect our spiritual belief in love.

Love in our work lives can present challenges, such as should we realize our potential by starting our own business if it might create financial insecurity? Should we give our all to supporting a coworker's potential, if it means that they get promoted over us? Should we accept the promotion that would require we move and risk creating distance with those we are attached to?

These are the types of conflicts that come up when we try to integrate our belief in love into our working lives. All the spiritual beliefs we have covered so far are there to prepare us to attempt the greatest of feats— living in love. It is in our ability to live in love that we prove whether or not we have integrated our beliefs in humility, surrender, discipline, gratitude, and connection. These preceding beliefs reduce distractions and fears so that we can awaken and refocus our attention on the limitless potential of life.

THE QUESTION: UNIVERSAL LOVE

Love was a beautiful idea I held as one of my spiritual beliefs, but things got messy when I attempted to integrate love into my daily life. It was one thing to love my child or close friend, but another to love that business competitor, difficult boss, or conniving coworker. It was one thing to love my spouse enough to celebrate their birthday, but another to love him enough to encourage his work passions, even if they took him away from our home more or changed our family's financial situation. I was quite willing to love myself enough to schedule a massage or take a vacation. Yet it was a whole new ball game when I needed to love myself enough to leave a high-paying, prestigious job to pursue the work I was meant to spend my sacred life doing.

Living in love is not the relaxed spiritual experience of watching doves soar and hearing choirs sing "Hallelujah." Living in love is the hardest thing we will ever do and yet it is infinitely rewarding. It is the path to whole and fulfilled living.

This chapter will focus specifically on deciding if you are ready to integrate your belief in love into your life and how that impacts your work. Like all the other chapters, I invite you to sit with our main question:

*Q: Have you integrated what you believe about
love into your life?*

But before we move on to what love does to your show,
reflect on what you believe about it. Is the following
statement what you believe?

*I believe that my highest purpose is to honor the
sacred gift of life. I reflect that honor by realizing
my own potential and supporting the potential of
others. I am most fulfilled when I am frequently
expressing, experiencing, and surrounded by love.*

For the purposes of integrating this belief, we are going
to explore the dimension of love that is not a feeling, but
an action. We are not talking about falling in love, but
rather what it means to live in love. Falling in love is a
fun and essential stage, but it is often rooted in what we
need and how we want to feel. The falling-in-love stage
has a purpose—it is there to pique our interest enough to
give us the time to form
a deeper connection.
Yet, it is not enough to
sustain a bond and cre-
ate space for spiritual
love. That is a decision
we have to make with
our actions.

**When we integrate
our belief in love, we
prioritize what honors
the potential of life
over how we hope
to feel.**

Living in love is when our thoughts, words, and actions align with treating ourselves and others with the reverence we have for the gift of life. Someone living in love is just as invested in others realizing their potential as they are in realizing their own. Someone living in love is broadly sharing their talents in the support of realizing the potential of all living beings around them.

Integrating a belief in love is how we engage in the broader show of life. Our most fulfilling work will flow from a life integrated with love. It is where we learn to produce our own work, but also how to support the potential of all characters.

When we are attached to the idea that we have to fight for our piece of the pie and needing certain outcomes, we cannot grant ourselves or anyone else the grace and freedom needed to pursue potential. And the great conflict of love is the decision point we will inevitably reach in all our episodes. Over and over again, we have to decide what is more important to us—holding on to our attachments or being strong enough to live in love.

THE CONFLICT

Every conflict creates a point of frustration that requires an outcome. Life will provide us with conflicts automatically, but we have a say in how we deal with them. Those living in surrender choose to observe their experiences instead of trying to control them, which makes the process more pleasant, but does not resolve the issue itself.

In Freytag's pyramid in Chapter 2, you'll see that conflict leads to the critical part of your show, as you are no longer building rising action and interest. We reach a climax whenever we need to choose a course of action to move on. In our work lives these can be small decisions such as whether to send an email and how to word it or larger questions about whether we should take a new job. Yet, our ability to work in love often stems from the lessons we learn in our personal lives.

Consider one of the more primal loving relationships— that of a parent and child. Almost instantaneously, a parent may be overwhelmed with a reverence for the gift of life that is embodied in their child. They want to see that gift fully realized. They work hard to align their thoughts, words, and actions to help that child realize their full potential. They honor their child's unique attributes and look for ways to bring out the best in them. Even when the child does things that would be unacceptable from anyone else (think waking you up multiple times during the night or throwing up on you) the parent offers grace and acceptance for where the child is in their journey. They recognize that though the child cannot meet *their* needs in this moment, they are still worthy of their love.

Loving parents recognize that they mustn't block this child's freedom to grow independently from them. They don't block them from learning to walk, and even help them, despite the fact that the child becomes less dependent on them by doing so. This encouraging of growth and freedom should go on and on until the child is grown. Even then, the parent watches and looks for ways to support. They may see their adult children stumble in life, and they are there to lovingly grant grace and support once again.

I understand that the above relationship example is only one form of living in love. You may not be a parent or perhaps you were raised with a different version of parental love. In this case, you might prefer to consider how living in love with your closest friend would appear in your show. With time, a bond forms between you. Information has been gathered, sometimes over many episodes and seasons, which forms a deep appreciation for the gift of life that is embodied in your dear friend. You value their life. You work hard to align your thoughts, words, and actions to help them realize their potential. You see and honor their unique attributes and look for ways to bring out the best in them.

When a friend does things that would be unacceptable from anyone else (says something insensitively or burdens us with their baggage—more than we can handle), we offer grace and acceptance for where our friend is on their journey. We recognize that though they cannot do better in this moment, they are still worthy of our love. We recognize that we mustn't stunt our friend's freedom to grow independently from us. We don't prevent them from building new friendships, making a move across the country, or pursuing a new business venture—despite the fact that it may threaten our attachment to them. We continue to grant them freedom and support them anyway. A good friend is continuously watching and looking for ways to support. When our friend stumbles in life (and they will) we look for ways to show grace and reflect back for them our view of their beautifully imperfect humanity.

> **EXERCISE**
>
> Grab your journal and answer the following questions:
>
> • Is this the kind of friend your character is?
> • Are these the kind of friends you have around you?
> • Is this how your belief in love is showing up in your life?

One last example and it is by far the hardest. Now we will revisit romantic love and see what "living in love" would look like in your show. For the purposes of the example, I am assuming that your lover is committed to you and that you have selected a kind, good character. If not, living in love with them and living in love with yourself will be impossible. We will get to that later.

For now, assume you have fallen in love and formed a quality connection. You have gathered information about your lover that has grown into a deep appreciation for the gift of life that they embody. You want to see that gift fully realized. You work hard to align your thoughts, words, and actions to help your lover realize the potential in their life. You honor their unique attributes and look for ways to bring out the best in them.

When your lover does things that would be unacceptable from anyone else—such as hurting your feelings or disappointing you—you offer grace and acceptance for where your lover is in their journey. You recognize that though they cannot do better in this moment, they are still worthy of your love. Once again, you grant them the same worthiness and acceptance we want for ourselves.

You recognize that you shouldn't prevent your lover's freedom to grow independently from you. You don't block them from expressing their natural personality or pursuing their passions, despite the fact that you may have to give up on some preconceived notions about what your relationship would look like. You continue to prioritize their freedom to be themselves and reach their potential over any attachment to an outcome.

You are constantly watching and looking for ways to support them. When you see your lover stumble in life (and you will have the closest view of their failures), you look for ways to grant grace and reflect back your view of their beautifully imperfect humanity. The reverence for the human potential of your lover never ends. The support for the human potential of your lover never ends. And the mere fact that you get to practice living in love supports your growth and potential.

By now, I'm sure you are seeing how hard living in love will be for your character. We have to work hard to love. It is difficult to keep granting grace when our feelings are hurt. It is challenging to grant freedom when we are attached and vulnerable. It is hard to resist trying to change someone into what we need instead of honoring their uniqueness.

The examples above work exactly the same way in loving ourselves. We are responsible for honoring our own gifts. When we fail to live up to who we want to be, we have to grant ourselves the same grace and acceptance. We recognize that though we can't do better in this moment, we are still worthy of love. We see and embrace the gift of wholeness that our spiritual path offers us. We don't limit ourselves or choose fear over growth. We don't try to change ourselves to be someone else. Instead we let our unique magnificent life flourish.

When you evaluate what "love" is based on the standards in the examples above, you will attract, evaluate, release, and retain mature loving relationships. Are you able to love others in this way? Are they able to love you in this way?

We cannot do much about who our family members are and what kind of love they are able to give. Sometimes they are simply incapable of providing this standard of love. But if you live this standard yourself, you will have more grace to give them and in doing so you will have more peace. You will grant them forgiveness and you will grant yourself the freedom to create boundaries where needed. But most importantly, by practicing integrating love into your life, you will support your own growth and potential. Living in love changes our immediate decisions and our future episodes.

In our intimate relationships, we have more say in choosing a partner and hopefully notice if the other person is incapable of maintaining love. Love doesn't develop immediately, nor without work. People don't change for love but living in love is transformational. This kind of love calls a higher being from within the person granting the love (you) and from the person receiving the grace and freedom to be whoever they truly are. I have seen miracles come about simply because one person in a relationship is able to give this kind of love while still loving themselves.

This brings us back to the conflicts in your show. Your conflicts will always be decisions of love or attachment. Which one will drive your actions? Love requires grace and freedom. Attachment requires judgment and manipulation. Love is hard work and poses great risks. Attachment forms effortlessly and is grounded in a desire for control and security.

Choosing to live in love is not the easy decision, but living our beliefs is not about choosing the easiest way to seek temporary happiness; it is about choosing to walk the spiritual path that leads to sustained fulfillment.

YOUR CHOICE: TO HONOR LIFE

Love is meant to reflect our value in the sacred gift of life. Honoring life comes more naturally when we are newly in love or serving in a caretaker role of a child. When love is the primary criterion, we weigh how our actions will impact the life of the other. We don't yell and scare the baby that just spit up on us. We value not scarring their natural personality with fear over making our displeasure known to them.

We know we love someone if we ask ourselves how our interactions are empowering or limiting their ability to be who they are supposed to be. We are honoring the gift of their life when we consider who they might be called to be, instead of who we need them to be or who we wish they were.

When my sons were infants I certainly wanted (and sometimes physically needed), a baby that slept through the night, wasn't screaming, and refrained from leaving me to clean up their spit-up and leaky diapers. Like most parents, I rarely got what I wanted or needed from my baby. And it was obvious to me that babies aren't able to give parents what they want or need. Babies aren't to blame for this, it is just where they are in their journey. My job was to love and support my babies anyway, so they could grow into whoever they might be.

To set our climax in love, we have to choose to shift our thinking away from evaluating our own feelings to supporting potential. Our thoughts need to move from

Living the belief of love necessitates that we consciously pause to consider how our every word, action, and decision honors the potential of life.

"how do I want to feel?" to "who am I called to be?" and "how can I help another become who they are called to be?"

In your show's episodes the climaxes are those real-life conflicts that your character must resolve. Break up or stay together? Is he/she a real friend? Should I go to this event? Where should I choose to live? Should I go back to school? Should I start this business?

As you observe these conflicts, the person living in love will consider only one question to drive the decision-making process: What decision helps me or someone else live authentically and experience the fullness of their potential? If the decision is about taking a new job, we ask ourselves:

- Will I "be" (not "feel") better because I took the job?

- Will this job move me closer to or fully allow me to show up in my professional life as my authentic self?

- Is it going to challenge me to engage with life more fully or might it make me comfortable and stagnant?

- Will taking this job impact the potential of anyone else?

There is nothing to fear when you make decisions from a loving place. Any decision made grounded in love will ultimately be the right one. It will be a decision we can be at peace with because we know it is aligned with our core spiritual beliefs and won't lead us astray. When we allow our human fears and motivations to drive our decisions it only serves to confuse, frustrate, and leave us second-guessing ourselves. It keeps us attached to a desire to control the outcomes and never at ease nor satisfied.

Love is the enabler of an integrated spiritual life and the only path to the work we are called to.

THE PATH OF LOVE

Living in connection and appreciating the living beings around you increasingly leads to love. You may choose to start that journey practicing on the people closest to you, but a spiritual belief in connection and love will eventually lead you to love broadly and freely.

Your show isn't about the life of your character. You are using gratitude and connection to create a story that has a broader view of your character in context with all other living beings. In addition to the conflicts you face, you will have conflicts about the state of our world and humanity itself. You are likely to grapple with real-life decisions and conflicts about where you sit on your political beliefs, when you choose to speak up or be silent, and how to volunteer your time or donate your money.

In addition to more deeply loving our romantic partners, families, and friends, we will have conflicts that require that we live in love at work with our clients, bosses, and coworkers. Taken further, living in love will lead us to conflicts that impact people we've just met and people we have never met but that seem to need our help.

On a personal level, love is the work of helping someone else realize their life's potential. Yet in your show, love is the work of helping humanity realize its potential. What is the life experience of others? How could it be better? What role could I play in providing for others' freedom and grace?

If you have been building a show that is integrated with your beliefs, these questions are as much a part of your episodes, as the questions that impact your character more directly. In both cases, the belief in love requires that you answer these questions with the highest respect for life. The benefit in paying attention to, and answering these questions, is that it will lead us in the direction of our highest work (more on that in Part II).

For now, just know that making better and clearer decisions is the gift of living in love. It takes complicated dilemmas and clarifies the path forward. The next step is to follow through on those decisions and live in power which is no small task either. That's coming up next.

CHAPTER 7

POWER

Power is a belief in our ability to tap into the soul's divinity to create our most authentic life. To live in power is to have the strength to direct our every action from a place of truth and transparency. When we live with power, we make the choices that attract our highest work and lead us to the unique experiences our soul is calling us to.

FINDING DISCERNMENT
AND COURAGE

In addition to working with people that are seeking new careers, I do a fair amount of work helping executives prepare for retirement. This is the phase of our lives when we assume we will have the most power over our daily experience. When we assume we will "be able" to do whatever we want—but that assumes we know what we want.

Most retiring executives have spent their entire working lives trying to accomplish objectives that measure their value in terms of profit and loss, promotions and bonuses. As they enter retirement, they are asked to consider how they will now measure the value of their time. More often than not, these executives have spent little time exploring what they truly enjoy doing in life and usually need a discovery phase, which can last anywhere from six months to two years, to discover their authentic motivations and passions.

During this phase, I recommend they suspend all judgment on what they think they should be doing and where they have seen other retired executives spend their time. Instead, I recommend creating a varied list of anything that might be of interest to them. From hobbies to leisure, charity work, teaching, for-profit and non-profit boards, and even new business ventures previously deemed too risky or time consuming. The purpose of this phase is to discover what their true feelings are, and not to start setting or pursuing new goals.

The plan is to start having conversations, reading articles, volunteering, and getting busy with the objective of discerning the value they derive simply from engaging in that activity. For the first time, they are not asking themselves if they could succeed in something, or if others will value their contribution, but seeking to discern their own truth about the value of their time. What do they want to be able to do? How do they want to use their power?

THE QUESTION: LOVE AND POWER

Love and power are inextricably linked. Choosing to live in love allows us to evaluate our conflicts and decide what we should do next. Living in power is having the discernment and courage to implement those decisions. If we value life, in the way we are spiritually called to, we won't wait until retirement to choose to live our truth. We will seek to integrate what we believe about power as a logical derivative of love.

Q: Have you integrated what you believe about power into your life?

Is this belief statement true or false for you?

I believe that I am connected to a powerful life force and I am most fulfilled when I have the confidence and strength to accept and live as my authentic self.

Do you believe that you have power? Do you believe you have a bond to a mighty spiritual force—one that calls you to live beyond fear to realize your full potential? Do you actually believe this to be true?

If not, the episodes we want to create will derail here. All our efforts to live our beliefs will be lost, if we cannot be brave enough to prioritize our truths over living in fear and attachment. Choosing to integrate any of our beliefs into our lives will be difficult. This work is not for the fainthearted. People living in their spiritual beliefs may appear kind and gentle—and they are. But I can assure you that anyone that has integrated their belief in love has been challenged to live with great power.

Integrating your beliefs into your life will mean making tough decisions and sometimes dealing with painful truths. That is where you'll need to harness and utilize the strength of power that lies within you.

POWER DAYS

In my exercise classes, we have something called "Power Days." These workouts build strength from the kind of movements we do most often in our daily lives—such as squatting, lifting, or stepping up—through *repetition*, *form*, and *effort*. The other notable aspect of Power Days is that we focus on exercises that create momentum—jumping, leaping, and thrusts. We are selecting exercises that prepare us for the activities we encounter frequently, but by adding momentum to them we increase our ability to do them with power.

My first few Power Days were extremely difficult. I had neither the strength to hold the proper form nor the ability to drive momentum. I stopped and started awkwardly throughout the workout to catch my breath and was inevitably sore the day after. There were days I considered calling in sick to work and not getting out of the bed post-workout. I was hurting that bad. I *didn't* feel powerful. The pain was worse because I was sore in the muscles I used most in my everyday life. Every time I tried to sit down, get up, or walk upstairs I was reminded how much my body ached. It was both *painful* and *inconvenient* to get used to these workouts. However, it got easier with each one and, over time, I built up strength, learned better form, and was even able to sustain momentum.

I'm sharing this story because living in power looks quite similar to a Power Day at the gym. Living in power is not about being loud or boisterous. It is also not about asserting control over others. Living in power is living a life with an emphasis on building spiritual strength through honest and transparent actions.

We can take every opportunity to increase our power to live our truth and practice better form while making life decisions. Living in power prepares us to be able to build an authentic life.

Our power grows every time we make a decision that is rooted in our truth. Having a firm commitment to truth is the only way to live in power. Our thoughts, words, and actions must be rooted in a commitment to being honest with ourselves and with others. This is easier said than done which is why it requires practice and strength.

Attachment and fear previously drove my decisions to hide or ignore my truth. I have made many career choices that ignored how I really felt. I have struggled to find contentment at points in my career when I was both reasonably good at my job and financially secure. My truth kept trying to tell me that I *wasn't* growing in a meaningful direction. But I was stuck living in attachment to the life I had already built. I *didn't want* to give up the safety of knowing what my professional future would look like.

Every Monday, my mind was consumed with convincing and justifying thoughts: *You can do this! It won't be that bad.* Every Friday, I couldn't wait to check out and unwind with a glass of wine: *It's over. Don't think about it again until Monday.* I tried to tell myself that I wanted the career I had, despite obvious signs that I did not.

Luckily, truth is strong and doesn't go down without a fight. Despite my best attempts to quiet it with logical justification, I needed to leave. I *wasn't* honoring my precious life nor my business partners by secretly being uncommitted to them. I was constantly choosing the weaker path of dishonest and inauthentic living.

When we live in love, we see how our decisions impact our potential and the potential of those around us. Using love as a guide helps us see what our truth is. Making decisions and doing the actions that implement that truth is how we live in power. But just like in my workouts, integrating power into our lives (especially in the beginning) will be both *painful* and *inconvenient.*

THE ACTIONS

How you address these conflicts is the falling action, as shown in Freytag's pyramid in Chapter 2. Falling action is where the problem, issue, or situation gets addressed, but not resolved, and shows the audience what the characters do in response to the conflict.

Your show's conflicts are decisions centered on what is best for the growth of everyone involved. When you write falling action with power, your characters are not afraid to be honest about what they think and feel. Your character cannot be afraid to see and live in a way that honors your truth. You continually make decisions that support your, and others', potential—even if those actions are painful and inconvenient.

In your show, living in truth day-to-day starts with aligning your character's smallest decisions with a commitment to truth and transparency. It is through these seemingly minor decisions that you will gain the strength to live in power when you need to make major decisions. Your character builds the momentum of power with a relentless commitment to the truth in each and every episode.

Telling the truth doesn't mean being brutal in our opinions or asserting our truth to be the same as fact. Being truthful only means getting into the habit of seeing and acting on what is true for us moment to moment. There will be times when what is true for us is simply not what we wish was true. There will be times that what is true for us is not the fastest path to growth, but seeing and

Living in truth and power has the ability to transform your life experiences. It is through revealing and honoring your truth that you attract and repel the people and situations you need to grow toward your work callings.

respecting that truth is part of honoring our lives.

Let's take a look at how your character would use their truth to strengthen their power from episode to episode. You will notice that no matter what the truth is for them, it is always possible to write the falling action with power. There is no *correct* or *best* truth only *your truth*. Please also keep in mind that this show is a comedy, so we will be approaching the conflict with lighthearted humor.

SCRIPT A

Season 1, Episode 1: What's for Lunch?	
Conflict	What should our character eat for lunch: the pizza or the kale salad? What supports and honors their life?
Truth A	Our character wants to eat healthier food and is ready to make different choices. This is what they see as the next step in their growth. Though they notice a craving for pizza, they believe they will best support and honor their life if they choose the kale salad.
	It is uncomfortable to make a different choice than they have in the past. They still see themselves as "someone who eats pizza," but they're flexible about releasing their attachment to their previous habits.
Falling Action A	Our character sees clearly what their truth is. There is no need for justifying or overanalyzing it. They select and eat the kale salad and feel good about it.
	This choice honors who they are right now and teaches them that they can trust themselves to live their truth—they are ready to try to change their eating habits starting with this lunch. They may not always choose the kale salad, but they will today. They will leave future food decisions to be decided by what their truth is in the future. They learn to trust themselves to honor their life one decision at a time.

SCRIPT B

Season 1, Episode 1: What's for Lunch?	
Conflict	What should our character eat for lunch: the pizza or the kale salad? What supports and honors their life?
Truth B	Our character is working to develop in other areas of their life and believes focusing on healthy eating as an additional goal right now would be too much pressure. It could derail their progress in other areas. Healthy eating is something they aspire to, but it is not a priority right now. What they want right now is a tasty meal that will indulge their senses. Though they wish they were ready to grow toward healthy eating, they are not. It will best support and honor their life if they choose to be truthful and eat the pizza.
Falling Action B	Our character sees clearly what their truth is. There is no need for justifying or overanalyzing. They select and eat the pizza with no regrets. This choice honors who they are right now and teaches them that they can trust themselves to live their truth—they are not ready to change their eating habits in this lunch. They may not always choose the pizza, but they will today. They will leave future decisions to be decided by what their truth is in the future. They learn to trust themselves to honor their life one decision at a time.

What to eat appears to be a simple decision. It is one we make several times a day but making the decision with a commitment to the truth increases our ability to discern what our truth even is and to trust ourselves to honor that truth with our actions.

If our character wants to choose the kale salad but chooses the pizza anyway because they are attached to seeing themselves as "someone who eats pizza," or are afraid they would never keep up the habit, they would have taught themselves that they do not honor their truth. In essence, they would have taught themselves that who they are right now and what is true for them is not worthy of being honored. And that is not living in power.

The same goes for the character that wants to choose the pizza. If they choose the kale salad anyway because they were attached to the thought that it is what they *should* do—even if it overloads them and derails their growth in other areas or they wanted others to see them choosing the kale salad, even if that isn't who they are right now—they would have taught themselves that they do not honor their truth. Once again, they would have taught themselves that who they are and what is true for them is not worthy of being honored. That is not power.

If you start from a place of love, only considering what will honor and encourage the potential of your life, you will know that you have your best interests in mind. From there, it doesn't matter what you choose. Any action you take rooted in power will be the correct one. Sometimes we are ready to grow in one area and other times we are not. The point of living in love is that we need to consider our potential and growth every single time.

When we keep our minds focused on honoring our lives we will grow eventually. Love makes sure we have our best interests and the interests of others in mind. Power allows us to act on that when we are truly ready.

EXERCISE

Grab your journal and reflect on your power as you answer the following questions:

- Are you living in power today?

- Are you committed to living in your truth?

- Are you able to see and act on that truth in both minor and major decisions? If not, what is holding you back?

YOUR CHOICE: TO STRENGTHEN YOUR TRUTH

It takes strength to see the truth. It takes practice to strengthen the muscles that help us live in truth. Similar to my early experience of Power Days, I was weak at the beginning. I had built significant portions of my life around partial truths, half-truths, things that were never true, and things that were no longer true. I did this because I wanted to please others, or hide who I actually was, in favor of trying to become the person I thought I should be.

If this is also the case for you, there is a good chance that your truth-telling muscles are weak at the moment. You haven't been exercising them regularly and don't know how to control your momentum just yet. That is perfectly understandable. Start by focusing on small decisions to begin building your power.

Power is having the ability to acknowledge, reveal, and act on your truth, whatever that might be. In practical terms, power is what it means to live authentically with those around you, but most importantly with yourself. We need power to say what we really mean. We need power to do what we really want to do. Love cannot manifest without the strength of power to follow through with our best intentions.

Choosing truth in your work life is not about choosing success. Sometimes it means choosing mediocre actions over perceived greatness. My truth means that sometimes I have to get off the track because I am not ready to run a particular race. Achievement is not the goal of integrating power. Being free to live authentically is. This is what aligns with our spiritual belief in our divine connection to a powerful life force, when we are powerful enough to honor our truth.

Ultimately, none of our work callings can be heard or followed without the guiding light of truth. To integrate a belief in power, we have to be honest with ourselves and tolerate the risks of transparency. This is easier to do if we wait until retirement. By then, the risks of doing what we want and being who we really are has fewer financial, and even social, implications. But if we are loving and honoring the gift of our precious lives, we are called to choose power as soon as we can. Why wait?

The process starts with small decisions like being ready to choose what you eat, what you will do tonight, if you'll do someone that small favor they asked, what you will wear tomorrow. We make those decisions far more often than we make large life decisions and how we make those choices teaches us whether we have *the ability to see* AND *the strength to honor* our truth.

Learning to see your truth will not only make you braver in the decisions that most affect you, it will also make you braver in the decisions that affect humanity as a whole. You will have the boldness to live with your spiritual beliefs and actions aligned. You will be a greater force for good. And that is what your show is actually about. That is why your character was created and how you will find your work. But it all starts with building power from the smallest of decisions until you are ready to make the larger ones.

Living your truth is a daily practice and a challenging journey. We will cover this in further detail in Part II, but for now think of it as a chain, linking your power with the creation of your life, and bridging the gap between your decisions and their outcomes.

Often times people reference that someone with great spiritual power appears to be full of joy and peace. They associate that happiness with living their beliefs. Though they are happy and peaceful they are also powerful. They are confident and brave enough to live in truth and show the world who they really are.

CHAPTER 8

PATIENCE

Patience is a belief in the spiritual journey being the only path to fulfillment and empowers us to release our human expectations for when opportunities will arise. When we infuse our work lives with spiritual patience, we are free to do our highest work with unshakable peace and trust that our life's journey will unfold appropriately.

MAINTAINING FOCUS

When asked what I do, I say that I support people during times of "career reflection" or "career transition." I make a point to separate the stages because they require a different focus.

Career reflection is when we pause to think through where our career is headed and consider the possible next steps. Someone going through a career reflection is almost always gainfully employed at the time. They tend to be content in their current role but question whether there will be future growth and work satisfaction in their current company, role, or even industry.

The work I do with this group seeks to align their passions and vision with a longer-term strategy and then define the next step in their career. Sometimes, clarifying what is important gives them the motivation to request a new role within their current company. Other times, our work provides the clarity they need to start networking and building relationships in a new area they want to pursue.

My goal in working with someone going through a career reflection is to make sure they keep their attention on what is important to them and don't get lost in their day-to-day activities and forget to drive their career in a more fulfilling direction. My job is to help them design and execute a networking strategy, to help make connections for them where I can, and keep them on my radar as I learn of new opportunities.

A career transition is when we are clearly in-between jobs or business opportunities and actively engaging in a full-time job search. A number of things can create a career transition but most often for my clients it arises from an executive downsizing due to mergers, acquisitions, or cost restructuring. Sometimes I work with individuals that have sold their businesses but aren't sure what to do next. Others pursue an active career transition because of a culture or expectation mismatch in their current job. They cut their losses and leave the job, so they can focus full-time on finding a better fit.

Most of my clients in these situations are privileged to have severance packages or other savings that cushion them from having to jump at any paying job, but there is still a sense of anxiety in a career transition that is not present in a career reflection.

My goal in working with someone going through a career transition is to help them balance securing their next role with the pursuit of something they will find fulfilling. My job is to help them gain clarity on what they want to do next and show them how to pursue it as aggressively as possible.

The key phrase in that last sentence are the words "as possible." A person in a career reflection finds it easy to be patient while busy and content in their current job. They trust the process. They can let their networking strategy progress at a natural pace. They can wait for the market to have opportunities that interest them. They are resilient to disappointment when interviews don't lead to an offer. They find it easier to be patient.

THE QUESTION:
PATIENCE—A MATTER OF TRUST

Integrating our beliefs focuses our thoughts and aligns our actions. We have looked at each belief closely and tried to discern why we struggle to implement it into our lives and whether we believe living it better would lead to fulfillment. Patience is the last belief but one we will use with great frequency. Trusting in the spiritual process of life is where integrating our beliefs will ultimately lead. We are challenged regularly to be patient and let our authentic lives, and therefore our authentic work, unfold.

Power is rooted in truth. Patience is rooted in trust. Patience is a state where we choose to trust in the process of life. We trust that life is inherently good and, though we may have ups and downs and find ourselves in unpleasant stages at times, it is all leading to a positive place. The process is leading where we want to go—to our most authentic and fulfilling life experience.

In the meantime, we are honest about what we can and cannot control. We trust the process enough to accept that the life we are currently living is the best we can do right now. To do that, we must recognize that the stages that cause us pain, uncertainty, or anxiety are also part of our growth. Patience is believing that there is a process to life, even when we cannot fully comprehend where it is leading us.

Q: Have you integrated what you believe about patience into your life?

Thinking about the question, is this statement true or false for you?

*I believe that my fullest life experience is worth
waiting for. I trust that if I live my beliefs I will
attract the opportunities I was meant to have. I
am most fulfilled when I am free from the pressure
of expectations and can be patient and at peace
while my life unfolds.*

If so, you will bring a different energy to your days—a
hopeful anticipation and a peaceful spirit.

A career transition has the same steps as a career
reflection, but a different energy and experience. My
clients in career transitions are anxious about where
opportunities will come from and when they will
materialize. I spend a great deal of my time explaining
and reinforcing the process that executive job searches
tend to follow, but also preparing them for the emotions
they will feel. Generally, the stages look something like this:

1. **Kick-off/prep**—feeling reasonably hopeful while
   defining targets, refining your career story, crafting
   and editing resumes, etc.

2. **Extensive networking**—feeling productive yet
   uncertain with some conversations leading to next
   steps and others going nowhere

3. **Waiting on opportunities**—feeling anxiety over
   the market and worrying that you'll get desperate,
   experiencing less activity and slower responses
   than you hoped for

4. **Interviewing**—feeling pressure as you prepare to do your best with some opportunities progressing and others ending

5. **Waiting on outcomes**—feeling a strong desire to finish your search, mixed with worry that you won't get the job or the offer you want most, mixed with concern that maybe you should hold out for other options and are rushing, mixed with impatience that the process has taken so long

6. **Offer negotiation**—feeling an overwhelming desire to finish the search and rest, but wanting to get the most possible during negotiation

7. **Celebratory announcements**—feeling relief and the beginning of hindsight that tells you every thing in the process happened for a reason

The purpose of explaining (and reinforcing) the process in advance helps executives anticipate and prepare for the unavoidable angst of uncertainty and delays. They cannot know when their efforts are leading somewhere, or when new opportunities will open up, and they cannot be sure they will be deemed a fit when they do. All of this creates greater anxiety in those going through a career transition because they desire a specific outcome as soon as possible. Yet that outcome takes time.

There are fewer executive roles in the market than other levels and, depending on the desired role, skillset, and geographic preferences, an executive search can take six months to a year or more, even when pursued aggressively. That's a lot of days to live with uncertainty and, while stress affects individuals differently, I've rarely worked with anyone that doesn't have a few days of doubt during their search and several bad weeks, if not months, is more usual. But while timing differs from client to client, they all ultimately land a new opportunity. In hindsight, everyone believes the ups and downs were a necessary part of the process that led them where they needed to be.

Spiritual patience is when we can be at peace with the episodes of our lives without knowing how our seasons will develop. We are at peace because we trust and honor the process enough to patiently follow wherever it might lead.

That is the gift of hindsight. We know the outcome, so we honor the process that lead us there.

THE RESOLUTION

Each episode of your show will highlight a storyline in your character's life. Some will have major events at the crux of the episode's climax. Should your character marry him/her? Should your character move across the country, or the globe, for a job opportunity? Other decisions will have smaller climaxes, such as the decision to accept a dinner invitation or volunteer opportunity. You may reach a climax over deciding when to clean out a closet or what to eat for lunch. What all these decisions have in common is how your character roots each stage in the belief process and uses those beliefs to make decisions about how you write your script.

At the end of each episode, you'll need to write the dénouement, as shown in Freytag's pyramid in Chapter 2. This is the end. This is how and where you'll finish each of your storylines to make room for the next episode. By the time you arrive at dénouement, your character will have run into an issue where they have to choose to honor life over attachment. You will have had to reveal to yourself (and others) what is true for you. Your character has exhibited incredible strength to get to this point. Choosing growth has simplified the decision and truth has deescalated the conflict. The last question is where should you go from here? How should you end the episode?

Your show is about a serious topic—the plight of all humanity. Yet, it is not a drama. We are purposefully writing a sitcom. Your goal is not to produce exaggerated emotion, but to amuse yourself and the audience. Your show will provide a good laugh over the mystery of life. You don't take conflict or your character too seriously. You are not here to figure it all out or make all the correct decisions. You are here to enjoy the experience.

In dénouement, you are writing the kind of quirky show that often leaves the resolution open for interpretation.

Your show forces each viewer to determine what the point of the episode is and wait to either confirm or reject their view in future episodes. In the episode "What's for Lunch?" with your character choosing the kale salad the audience is left to ask themselves:

Did your character choose the kale salad because you are going to be a salad-eater and so humorously annoy others with your healthy choices in future episodes?

OR

Was that decision a lead-up to a funny future episode where you grow tired of kale salad, start hating salads, and end up eating an entire carton of ice cream?

OR

Was that kale-salad decision there to help grow your self-control, but in the overall story healthy eating is not a primary goal this season?

In all of these outcomes, lessons will be learned, and the audience will be amused. Character development will occur and your character's motivations (truth) will be further revealed through your actions. There are multiple future episodes that can be imagined, but the audience has to have patience because they cannot be sure where all this is going. They cannot be sure if your character is forever changed or just experimenting with change. They have to trust the process and accept that the episode is over, but the season is ongoing.

Either way, you will try to have interesting and funny episodes. That will make it worth the audience's time just to experience the show. They can trust that the writers of the show will string episodes together properly with a mix of opportunities for your character to grow and have mostly amusing experiences. Growth and goals in your episodes do matter, but never forget that a show about the gift of life should be joyful. If life is indeed our greatest gift, then seek the potential for joy in your episodes.

TRUSTING THE PROCESS

We will write the dénouement for the episodes of our lives with this in mind. We do the work to be the writers, but we live out the episodes as if we are in the audience. We are working to focus on our spiritual growth while living a lighthearted and enjoyable experience. The questions are:

- Can you peacefully create the episodes of your life without needing to know what opportunities are coming your way?

- Can you learn to enjoy your days one episode at a time?

Integrating patience allows our conflicts to feel resolved, even when we cannot see how our future episodes will be written. We own our part in the current episode without trying to predict what the seasons of our lives will look like. We trust in the process of living our beliefs to lead us to fulfillment.

The resolution of our conflicts comes whenever we realize that we are making spiritual progress regardless.

We are not sitting around waiting for life to come to us. We are actively but patiently building our lives, one episode at a time.

It is when we can enjoy our experiences and trust the process that we can rest in knowing that we are doing all we can do in any given moment. Peace is the by-product of patience.

Being who your character wants to be means peacefully doing all you can do. You don't do more than you can do or less than you can do. If you cannot do more right now, you'll see the truth in that and wait for the episode when you can. If you can do more, you'll see the truth in that and commit to those actions regardless of where they might lead. That is the continuous process of living in patience—truth, trust, and peace.

YOUR CHOICE: TO TAKE ACTION

On a practical level, our integrated beliefs so far have given us a process that looks something like this:

1. We commit to living our beliefs to the best of our ability. We understand that it will never result in perfection, but it will result in living authentically with increased joy, courage, and resilience.

2. Once rooted in our beliefs, we commit ourselves to continuously seek to live with an open heart and open mind so that we might clearly discern what is true for us in any given moment.

3. We align our actions (what we do and do not do) with our truth. That means doing things when we are ready and not doing them when we are not ready.

4. We trust the process of life and are at peace with any result that comes. We trust that it will take us on the journey that we are meant to be on. We trust that it will take us at the pace that we are meant to travel.

This journey may include doing things from a place of truth that cause us temporary pain. The pain may make us anxious about the process. But we will trust it anyway. It may also include what appears to be mistakes or detours. We will give up the anxiety and pressure of having to make the "correct" decisions in the hope of creating the perfect life. Instead, we commit to be patient with the process and stay on our perfect journey.

No matter what exercise routine you choose, it takes time for the body to strengthen and adjust to new activities. That will also be the case as you begin to embed your beliefs more fully into your daily decisions. At first, our strength around a belief may be weak. Practicing that belief will feel unfamiliar. Making the initial attempts to embed that belief in our thinking and behavior may be awkward and quickly cause us frustration or fatigue. This too is a natural part of the process. Over time however, we strengthen our muscle memory. It becomes quicker to orient our minds to the belief. We gain better form which makes us use the belief more efficiently. It gets easier to do the daily actions that reflect what we believe. Most importantly, we can use our strength to live in that belief without fatiguing as quickly. Eventually, we can live out the actions of our beliefs without enduring as much pain and recovery time.

Unfortunately, no matter how much we exercise, there is no way of making our muscles invincible. A fact of biology is that strength helps us to use the body with greater resilience and efficiency, but we must accept that the human body is forever fragile and vulnerable. We continue to strengthen it because we want to use it with greater power and enjoy a faster recovery. We know that we cannot predict issues nor create an invincible body just because we are stronger. We have to trust that strength is better than weakness. We have to trust in the truth that a healthy body creates the best life experience.

Living in patience means trusting that a stronger belief system for guiding our daily decisions will lead to our best life experiences. As long as we follow our truth, we will be exactly where we need to be for the moment. We will be doing the correct things and on the correct journey. Our thoughts will orient toward asking first "What is my truth?" instead of jumping right into action. We will ask the question and patiently wait for however long it takes to get the answer.

Patience is an action. It is something we must think and do, like all the other beliefs. Patience isn't an inactive posture that makes us a spectator in our own lives. We may be forced to wait out certain circumstances, but we always play an active role in how we pass the time.

EXERCISE

To support you in integrating patience, use this mantra whenever anxiety or pressure starts to build. Find a quiet moment and say to yourself:

"I trust that the right opportunities are coming my way, and I trust in the process of life."

In the beginning, use this mantra each morning (especially on work days) or whenever you need a reminder.

TRUST THAT THE TRUTH WILL REVEAL ITSELF

Many times, I have chosen to search for alternative ways to speed up a process or overanalyze things with the kind of vigor that highlights a lack of peace. If we choose to live in patience, we have to make an active choice to do so. We have to make an active choice to rest in the idea that the process will steer us in the right direction. We will have to repeatedly redirect our minds from ways to accelerate our plans to ways to connect with our truth and live it.

Patience is trusting that your truth will reveal what you should be doing or when you should be doing nothing. Your growth has to unfold throughout your life, but you cannot predict or control the exact timing and order of the path. At the beginning of our journey, surrender taught us to stop trying to control life, but patience is where we actually do the work of trusting and waiting. This work happens moment to moment. Trusting in the process means not trying to skip steps, rush, or jump ahead, but also not failing to take the steps when it is time. Patience is valuing the process enough to wait for whatever comes next.

This has major implications in the work of our lives. For me, integrating patience brought up questions, such as:

- Did I leave that job in haste and should I have stayed a little longer?
- Should I have taken the first new role offered or held out for the right thing?
- Did I fail to follow a passion or take a risk because I couldn't predict the outcomes?

My lack of love, power, and patience has cost me plenty in my career to date, but no longer. I am now committed to trusting the process and following the truth wherever it leads. Are you ready to make that same leap? Have you already done so, or would you like to start now?

THE STORY CONTINUES...

Part I was about taking time to integrate your beliefs, and made you the producer and writer of your own life. It is important to think about what kind of show you want to live in and how you want to write your episodes before moving on to exploring your individual character. Your beliefs create the show that will lead to your truest and best life experience.

Can you imagine watching a show where the actors showed up with no idea about what the show was supposed to be about? It would certainly lack consistency in quality and experience. Where the show went from episode to episode and season to season would be heavily influenced by the actors' fluctuating moods, rather than grounded in the producer's vision. We would not enjoy watching this show but might keep asking, "What is this show supposed to be about?" and never get an answer.

Through your reflection in Part I, you have set the stage for the show you want to create. I hope you feel grounded in not just what the overall show is about, but how you will practically approach each episode in order to integrate your beliefs.

In Part II, we will explore what it means to be the actors and actresses in our lives. You have a show concept and a script, but now you need to arrive on set and play your character. And so our work in the next part of the book is to anchor our lives in what we believe which leads us to our highest and most fulfilling work.

PART II

ANCHORED

an•chor (aNGkər)

verb

1. Secure firmly in position.
2. Provide with a firm basis or foundation. Past tense: anchored; 3rd person present: anchors; present participle: anchoring.

CHAPTER 9

IDENTITY

Identity defines how we view ourselves, who we think we are, and what we think we are capable of. Our deepest beliefs anchor our identity with either our human selves or our souls. *Who am I?* is the fundamental question leading us to our highest work because our spiritual selves are not bound to the limits of the world. Our spiritual selves will chart a bolder course and know that we are empowered with infinite potential.

LEARNING TO TRUST YOURSELF

Have you ever felt unable to trust that your work decisions were the ones you truly wanted? I certainly have. There were times when I was too stressed, overworked, or anxious to escape a bad boss to direct my next steps appropriately. Distraction, exhaustion, or anxiety had disconnected me from my spiritual self. I *didn't* trust that version of me to lead me to the work I was called to do. I knew that the person I was in my mind at that moment wouldn't make the decisions the person I am in my soul desired.

This is a common problem for my clients as well. They come to me fresh off a long and hard season of tireless (and sometimes unfulfilling) work ready for a change, but they sense that they are not the best version of themselves to start making decisions. Before we even get started with working on their resume or networking plan, I counsel them on ways to reconnect with themselves before making any work choices.

If they have the luxury of taking a vacation, travel can broaden their exposure to life and stimulate their spiritual connection. When travel isn't an option, the important thing is to take time to reconnect with the joys of their life. To stop strategizing about their career, and instead use the time to rediscover the things that make them feel grounded and alive. Common life-affirming pursuits are time spent with family, time dedicated to hobbies, enjoying nature, or laughing with friends over a delicious meal. The purpose of this time is to activate their higher being, so they'll be prepared to place their spiritual self in the roles of director, evaluator, and decider of their work choices.

THE QUESTION:
IDENTIFY WHO YOU ARE

In Part I, the journey of integrating our beliefs started with a question of humility. Integrating humility focuses our lives on more than just our own experience, but on the equal and miraculous gift of all souls. It was the first belief we covered and has the largest impact on all of the others. There is no point in trying to live in connection or love, if we can't expand our focus beyond our own needs, wants, and desires. We'll never be able to place the highest value on the gift of life, and let that drive us toward realizing our potential, if we can't integrate our belief in humility.

The same is true for the first question we will be answering in Part II, which I hope will anchor your real-world work in your spiritual life. Therefore, the first question this chapter asks us to consider is who we are bringing to this process. What version of yourself do you want to be making your decisions? Specifically, the question I invite you to reflect on as we move through this chapter is:

Q: Is my identity anchored in my beliefs?

"Who am I?" or rather who am I supposed to be based on my beliefs? The answer to this question has implications for all the chapters to come. Often when we think about "who we are," we come up with a perception based on two things—our outward identity and our inward ego.

Yet a life anchored in our spiritual beliefs requires that we identify with more. So, what *does* it mean to be a spiritual being and to live with our identity anchored in that understanding? How does that spiritual being better prepare us for our work?

There are basic facts that we may use to identify who we are. These are things like:

- Age
- Gender identification
- Race
- Nationality
- Physical impairments
- Religion
- Sexual orientation
- Personality traits
- Social and class rankings
- Affluence or lack thereof

These facts are neutral in meaning, but we place our own biases and value judgments on what they mean for our identity. Here is an example of how our identity can be shaped differently with the same facts. Imagine a 49-year-old single, heterosexual woman from France, who is a Catholic, and also blind.

PERSON A'S PERCEIVED IDENTITY:

- 49 is still rather young. I am young.
- France is a great place to be young and single. I am where I need to be.
- Women are emotional. I am too emotional.
- Blind people are more creative. I am creative.
- Catholics are kind and compassionate. I am kind and compassionate.

PERSON B'S PERCEIVED IDENTITY:

- 49 is past your prime. I am old now.
- France is a hard place to be single. I am stuck in the wrong place.
- Older women are practical. I am practical.
- Blind people are better listeners. I am a good friend because I am a good listener.
- Catholics are rigid and strict. I am too stuck in my ways.

Two people can come up with entirely different interpretations of what their identity is using the same facts. This is because our preconceived ideas of what each identification category means colors our viewpoint of our capabilities. It impacts our work when we consider:

- Is this person old and out of time for new crazy pursuits or is she young with ample energy and decades of time to launch a new work platform?

- Is being a woman a reason to assume her desires to make a change are merely an emotional response that should be dismissed, or should she trust in her ability to be pragmatic in her approach and explore new endeavors?

Knowing our factual categories isn't enough, we have to know what our biases around who we are translate into. We have to know what kind of traits and destinies we may unconsciously be tying our identity to.

EXERCISE

Take out your journal and consider the following question:

What stories are you telling yourself about your identity and how are they empowering or limiting your work life?

Think about your own characteristics. They do not need to be limited to the ones I have chosen below. Think of anything that is relevant to you. Write them all down. Here are some categories to consider:

- Age
- Gender identification (or lack thereof)
- Race

- Nationality
- Religion
- Sexual orientation
- Height
- Weight
- Body type
- Relationship status
- Family history
- Education
- Income level
- Occupation
- Hobbies

These are just a few to get you started but add anything to your list that you identify with. Things you think it would be important for someone to know if they were going to take over from here and live life as you.

As you look at your list, consider what judgments you have put on each descriptor. What does it mean *to you* to be categorized as your race? To be from your country of origin? To have your income? To wear your clothing size? What is the story for good or bad that you have created about your identity? This story impacts who you think you are.

We will spend the rest of this chapter focusing on how an identity anchored in our spiritual beliefs transcends these categories, but I won't pretend that dealing with these outward traits, and the stories we tell ourselves about who we are in the human world, isn't worth exploring as well.

When we are anchored in our spiritual beliefs, we are in touch with the glorious, infinite nature of the life force inside of us. That version of ourselves, if we truly believe it exists and firmly anchor our identity to it, is capable of great feats and daring work endeavors. That version of ourselves isn't tied down to the perceptions we may already have of our identity. So the more we anchor our identities with our spiritual being, the more we are able to release and redefine the negative perceptions we have around our human identity. I can't emphasize enough the impact this can have on how we will choose to show up in the world, the decisions we make, and the kind of work we can get done in our lives.

YOUR CHARACTER

Your characteristics and traits are easily identifiable. Any actor playing your character will need to know what those traits mean to you. Yet, those categories can be distractions that our ego uses to keep us from connecting with our souls. They can leave us focused on the things that separate us from others and become distorted from our biases and insecurities.

IDENTITY

We are our souls above all else. In your show that means something powerful for your work. It means that you are whole and worthy already—right now despite any perceived imperfections. When we are anchored in an identity based on our spiritual being, we are equipped to live out the script that will help us realize our highest potential and fulfillment. Your character must connect with, and reflect, that identification with your spiritual self. That is who your character was written to be.

UNDERSTANDING YOUR CHARACTER

The next step in the process of creating your show is to explore your character. It is time to act out your part on the stage of life. To do that well, you'll need to align the show you have created with your character's identity. We are building a life and playing a character whether we actively create that character or not. Instead you may be showing up every day and playing your part without any idea of the type of show you want to live in nor who your character should be.

Konstantin Stanislavski was born in 1863. For 75 years, his character was on the stage of life. The legacy of his work continues today. The famous Russian playwright is widely credited as the father of modern acting methods. Most acting techniques have some derivative of Stanislavski's system. Actors spend their lives trying to understand and perfect his methods. We will be merely skimming the surface of his approach to acting in the chapters that follow.

Instead of seeing acting skills as "fixed" or "natural" talent, Stanislavski's system showed that realistic acting was a discipline that could be practiced and improved. For our purposes, we will be using the seven questions he believed each actor should ask themselves to understand their character's role:

- Who am I?

- Where am I?

- What time is it?

- What do I want?

- How will I get it?

- Why do I want it?

- What must I overcome to get what I want?

Not every character in our show will find and pursue their highest work. Many people die never feeling as if they lived up to their full potential. They die wondering if their lives should have been different or if they could have done more with their gifts.

Your perception of your character's identity is relative because we don't view the facts (e.g. our gender, race, etc.) in real terms. We use those categories to make relative judgments on the value of our traits based on our own experiences and how we view the world. It is similar to each actor creating a character differently. Actors draw from their own experiences and emotions to decide what their character might think, say, and do.

Yet, characters are identifiable no matter who plays them. Lady Macbeth is always some version of who we expect her to be on stage. A script guides her words and actions, and also creates consistency in the character portrayal.

Anchoring your character to your spiritual beliefs is meant to provide the same structure of a script in life. If you have been living without doing the deliberate work of being the producer and writer of your life, you have been living without a script. Your identity and ego are the only things that have been creating your character.

Thankfully, we know what our show is about. Each episode has a script to follow. As any actor trained in Stanislavski's system, we will study that script closely to get a better sense of who our character is and should be. Here is a refresher on what you learned about your character through the show design and script-writing process in Part I.

Guiding Belief	Show/Script Decision	Character Implication
Humility	Topic: All of humanity	There is no main character and your character sees themselves as equal to everyone else.
Surrender	Genre: Comedy	Your character focuses on humorously observing their life experience.
Discipline	Format: Sitcom series	Your character evolves and re-creates themselves through repeatable actions from episode to episode.
Gratitude	Exposition: The episodes begin by exploring not just what your character is blessed to experience but what they do not have to endure.	Your character approaches their days seeking to gain greater context on their privileges.
Connection	Rising action: Actions leading up to the climax create greater opportunity for characters to interact and deeply connect with each other.	Your character orients their days to seek out and gain understanding and compassion for others.

Guiding Belief	Show/Script Decision	Character Implication
Love	Climax: All conflicts for the episodes will be decided based on what honors the gift of life.	Your character honors the gift of life. They grant grace and acceptance to themselves and others. They work to fully utilize their gift and support the potential in the lives of others.
Power	Falling action: Characters respond to decisions and conflicts with the courage to see and act on what is true for them in that moment.	Your character is not afraid to live out their true feelings at all times and reveal that truth with their words and actions.
Patience	Dénouement: Episodes end with decisions but leave open many possibilities on where the story will lead from season to season.	Your character trusts the process of living in their beliefs. They can wait patiently to see how their individual episodes impact the seasons of their life.

EXERCISE

With this framework in mind, who does your character need to be? Spend a few moments, journaling your thoughts.

We have done a lot of work to align our lives with our spiritual beliefs because we believe that fulfillment is found when we live complete and whole in the human world, fully identified with our spiritual self. To be spiritually whole is to bring all parts of yourself together as one; to bask in the glory of your spiritual self, while knowing your potential limitations, previous mistakes, and future obstacles. It is to create a show that is rooted in the daily episodes of real life, while actively manifesting a character that is always identified with the spirit within them. This spirit is what keeps us connected to the whole, worthy, and complete life force that is powerful enough to manifest work that matters.

Our spiritual identity empowers us to do all the things that our human self doubts we are capable of.

We need a character that can make work decisions from their soul. We need a character that respects the power and beauty of the soul enough to honor their own life's potential and the life potential of others. Your character can separate him or herself from their mind's fears and analysis to observe their soul's truth.

As we continue to move deeper into Part II, you'll be creating a character that is connected enough to their God-given soul to know that they're capable and worthy of doing meaningful work. The ego tries to trick us into believing that we are our minds and nothing else. It tries to get us to ignore the soul and identify only with the mind.

Your ability to live anchored to your soul's perfection enables you to show up as the character your show intends you to be. Our soul is beautiful, powerful, and worthy despite any journey our mind may be taking us on. The path to your highest work starts with appreciating that you are whole already.

When your character can believe in their spiritual wholeness, you can anchor your work in your beliefs. When you show up in each episode already whole, you stop giving so much attention to trying to hide or fix yourself and let your work journey play out with patience.

YOUR CHOICE:
TO DEEPEN YOUR SPIRITUAL PRACTICE

My intention in this book is to lay out a logical framework that connects our beliefs to our work. However, identifying with the wholeness of your soul is not a logical process that will take place in the mind. It is not a process that words can adequately explain. It is derived from your spiritual practice and *has to* be experienced independently of this book.

Wholeness is inherent in spiritual life. It is the power you receive from your spiritual connection to God, the universe, or creation (however your practice categorizes it). Growing our spiritual connection has to be done on our own through prayer, praise, meditation, study, time in nature, or whatever else helps us tap into the spiritual realm.

Connecting our identity to our spiritual self is critical to making work decisions. We will fail to pursue the paths we are most called to if our identity is not anchored in a deep connection to our soul and a sense of wholeness.

We use our spiritual path to experience a connection with God and identify with the spirit within us. It is that connection that will allow us to appreciate and live in the wholeness of our soul.

Your soul is worthy despite any mistakes you have made in the past, despite the people you have hurt, the thoughts you have had, and the failures that still lie ahead. The connection to your soul reminds you that you are still worthy of living your fullest life experience and manifesting your best life's work.

If you are wondering what anchoring your identity in your spiritual self would look like, the best place to start is through your preferred spiritual practice and to spend some time going deeper on your spiritual path. All spiritual practices such as prayer, meditation, worship, or study are designed to strengthen your understanding that the life force within you is connected to a powerful source of creation, peace, and resilience. Any spiritual path you choose to follow will lead you to wholeness.

When you feel that connection for yourself and identify who you are as a spiritual being, you can trust that you are worthy of working whole simply because you are a magnificent living being. It takes your beliefs from being something you understand to something you can anchor your entire life in.

Anchoring in our beliefs takes sustained effort to connect with the spiritual world. It takes sustained effort to continue feeling and remembering that connection, as we live out our daily conflicts and episodes. Once you fully identify with your spiritual being you will be ready to start living and working whole.

Working whole means being willing to accept miraculous work assignments that allow us to be a conduit of God's love without feeling fraudulent or hypocritical. None of us are perfect. There are many things that I have done that I regret. There are many times that I haven't lived up to my beliefs. But, my story is not unique, and despite my best efforts I will fail again. Yet, that cannot hold us back from staying identified with our whole, beautiful, and brilliant spiritual selves enough to get our work done in this life.

It is our wholeness that anchors our lives and opens us up to hear our highest callings. Wholeness frees us to stop seeking a perpetual need for validation and achievement, so we can shift our focus to doing meaningful work.

CHAPTER 10

ENVIRONMENT

The surroundings and conditions in which we live define our environment, and have a profound impact on the work of our lives. Where we choose to place ourselves, and how we define the boundaries of our environment, shapes who we are and the kind of work we will pursue.

EXPANDING OUR HORIZONS

Most of my work involves giving career advice to people at the senior end of their careers. I've also spent over a decade as a volunteer working with high school and college students. My goal is to help them shape their future work from the very beginning. The needs of these two groups couldn't be more different. One has more time and ability to shape the environment of their work lives, as a high school student has all of their career decisions ahead of them. They could do absolutely anything, which is both an exciting and daunting place to be. A senior executive has already made a series of decisions that have built deeper skills and brought accomplishments. Yet, each decision has narrowed their path and it is difficult to change directions at that point. They tend to be more secure in their careers, but often yearn for greater flexibility.

Despite the differences in these two groups, the same question shapes their trajectory: How far to push outside their comfort zone. These questions come to me in a variety of ways. The ones I hear from the senior executives are:

- How do you know when something is a doable stretch opportunity or just a bad idea?

- I'm fine to get out of my comfort zone, I've done it many times. But, how much is too much?

- Between us, I'm both flattered that they think I can do this and nervous. The offer is a good one, but what are my options if I fail? How will it impact the rest of my career?

The students ask their questions differently, but with the same emphasis. I hear things like:

- Should I pursue what I'm already good at or what I enjoy?

- If I change majors and don't do well, how much will that impact my future?

- Should I pursue an industry that is easier to break into or the one I love?

Either way, the questions boil down to a choice about whether they should choose to put themselves in an environment that is riskier but will challenge them to grow, or if they should choose a safer, more comfortable path.

THE QUESTION: CHOOSING YOUR ENVIRONMENT

Seeking comfort in our work environment can take on many shapes and forms. There are job opportunities that may place us in a new geography that will expand our understanding of the world. But there are also geographies where we will be more comfortable. Which one should we choose?

We may have to decide between working with individuals that push us to expand our world view, leadership style, or communication skills, but those will not be the people we are most comfortable being around. And certainly, the jobs themselves can stretch us. That is where we get the term "stretch assignment," meaning a job that is a leap above what we've previously done and requires that we expand our skills, and so is riskier and can be quite uncomfortable, especially in the beginning.

Rarely do I work with someone that is more anxious than a highly accomplished leader deciding to accept an offer to be a first-time CEO. They have worked their entire career to reach this point and be the top boss. But excited as they may be, they understand that their work environment is going to be quite uncomfortable and the stakes will be high.

So, the question of this chapter is one of environment. What kind of environment should we be placing ourselves in based on our spiritual beliefs? How will our decisions around expansion and comfort impact the work of our lives? As we explore this topic, keep in mind your question for this chapter:

Q: Is my environment anchored in my beliefs?

LIVING IN THE BUBBLE

Our spiritual beliefs call us to live in reverence of the sacred and amazing gift of life, which means that we have to do the work to immerse ourselves in life as much as possible. We have to open ourselves to the vulnerability of leaving our comfort zone, but the reward is an expansion of capabilities, perspective, emotional capacity, and resilience.

I have a close friend that calls her hometown, "The Bubble." She calls it that not as a negative statement, but as a reflection for how the town tends to shield her from experiencing issues and problems happening in other parts of the country and world. This Bubble is recognized as a desirable place to live with its strong public education system and diverse communities living in harmony together. There is prosperity and a culture of community service. They have access to nature and the arts. Their job market is stable and thriving.

It is not a perfect town and there are people that struggle there, but for most it is a comfortable place to live and work. It is a lovely environment to find yourself in and bubbles often are. If we were uncomfortable in our bubble, we would break out of them easily. We stay in them because they are stable and safe.

The spiritual problem with living in a bubble is that we can lose touch with the broader life experience. It is easy to build up blind spots about what others need, feel, or struggle with, if all we see is one narrow data set. We may be comfortable living in our bubble, but we may be missing an opportunity to live what we believe.

When we anchor our environment in our spiritual beliefs we seek first to broaden our engagement with life. There are physical environments that can expand our engagement and there are mental and emotional environments that do the same. What these have in common is that they will be new to us at first. They will require that we choose to expand our perspective over staying comfortable.

Now, I am not going to pretend that this is easy, which is why we have to be anchored in our identity with our spiritual being, as we explored in the previous chapter. We cannot anchor our environment in our beliefs until we identify fully with our soul. Our human self loves comfort and avoids vulnerability because it makes us feel afraid or deficient. But our soul is already complete and whole. Our spiritual being is undiminished by vulnerability and we empower it to guide our work when we are open to the full experience of life.

Our ability to set our lives in the broader world allows us to gather data from new environments that will most certainly lead us to new places.

Anchoring our physical, mental, and emotional environment in our spiritual beliefs has huge implications on our ability to identify the work callings that will be most fulfilling to us. Working whole frees us from focusing on what we need from the human world to begin seeing what the spiritual world might be calling us to.

YOUR SETTING

A script tells the actor who their character is, but also where their story is set. The actor then considers how their character feels about that place. Is it safe or dangerous? Is it a public or private place? Your character will act differently based on how you perceive and feel about your surroundings.

Our script is about humanity so there may be scenes set in our home, city, or work, but these locations are not the main setting of the entire show. The script places your character with a focus on their entire life experience, which means the show will be set outside of their immediate surroundings. How does your character feel about where they are?

When you turn on a TV show the setting is likely the first thing you notice. Is it in a dark alley? Are we in someone's living room? Does this place look comfortable? Is it a place set up for romance or battles?

At first, I found it hard to set my show in the broader life experience. There were so many things about life that I frankly wanted to avoid. The more I paid attention to it, the more I saw the pain and suffering around me. I had problems and conflicts of my own and saw my emotional capacity as full. Perhaps like me, you have life circumstances (illness, grief, heartache, failure, etc.) that are quite consuming on their own. Perhaps you have a calendar packed full of obligations. Maybe your own suffering feels insurmountable and you are barely coping. Sometimes I felt that I had too much on my own plate to add someone else's pain. I felt unable to be who my character was supposed to be.

Without living the script of our beliefs, it can be too high of a hurdle to find the space to expand our emotional capacity. It can be hard enough being grateful amidst our own daily struggles. We may not want to add any additional conflicts into our environment. Without our script, we may wish to engage more with life, but it is so much easier to stay in our bubbles.

When we anchor our environment in the broader world, we set ourselves up to find the work callings we are passionate about. It may feel like we are subjecting ourselves to unnecessary discomfort, but it is precisely this data that can lead us to work we never considered. Doing meaningful work will mean something different to everyone, but it all starts with discovering what moves us the most.

Anchoring our environment in the broader world helps us explore and find the mission we most want to start working in service of.

Let's explore a few examples of how your character's setting might play out. Consider the scene below.

SEASON 38, EPISODE 13725
(TUESDAY IN JULY)

Your character goes online to check their social media feed and sees that a friend has shared two very different posts. One post is an article about the astounding level of violence in the streets of Chicago the previous weekend. The other is about kicking off her day with an iced coffee from Starbucks. Same person. Same hour. How will your character engage?

This happened to me in real life and I have to admit to engaging only with the Starbucks post at first. It was fun, light, and relatable. I had just left Starbucks myself.

I am not from Chicago. I have been there several times on work trips, but I don't know the city well. Also, the Chicago post made me feel sad and helpless. I scrolled past it at first and only came back to it out of guilt. I knew what the story would say before I read it—random violence in a poor neighborhood. Things are getting worse. Many dead.

This article *wasn't* in any way uplifting. I read nothing that made me hope things would get better. Was that a waste of time? Was that a pointless drain on my positive outlook? Was that a needless distraction to my otherwise pleasant Tuesday morning?

Our script would say no, because your character is trying to actively seek out the truth in the human experience. Your character is aware that they play a role in the greater life experience and how they choose to show up and play that role matters.

Media outlets, local politicians, CEOs, and world leaders have become increasingly sophisticated at noticing what large groups of people care about and making decisions based on that knowledge. They notice that many of us care about celebrity stories. We care about feel-good rescue efforts. We care about the untimely deaths of people that are supposed to live in safe areas and not supposed to die young. We care about fame and fortune, and the showmanship of political fights. We definitely care about consumer products (hence the Starbucks post). And you better believe we care about anything that involves "winning" from sports to business to politics.

So those are some of the things that large groups of us definitely do care about. What are some things we appear to care less about?

If the data is correct, we don't seem to care as much about people dying in poor neighborhoods. Or people dying in parts of the world we already assume are unsafe. I won't pretend that racial and religious bias is not also a factor in what we care about, but for the ordinary compassionate person living in a comfortable bubble, it has more to do with capacity. Our emotional capacity is limited, and our vulnerability muscle is weak, so we choose to only engage with the things that hit closest to home.

To anchor our environment to our spiritual beliefs, your character must answer the question, "Where am I?" This will require enduring the discomfort of leaving the bubble and engaging in the broader world.

You may be surprised to know the kind of impact what you choose to let into your environment has on the overall show. For starters, people in positions of power (within business, media, and politics) spend hours tracking and analyzing the numerical data on what we are paying attention to. They know what we click on and what we don't. They closely track what we do on social media sites. They know if we share or retweet a post or simply "like" it. The difference illustrates a greater level of agreement with the content. They even know if we stayed on the page long enough to actually read the article or if we quickly left. That is called the bounce rate. They may know if we ran any follow-up searches on the topic. They know if more people than normal are sending emails with the word "Chicago," "climate change," or "Syria." Even offline, people are gathering data on what organizations are focusing on. Over the course of your regular day, you may be unknowingly part of a study on what is being overheard in grocery stores or coffee-line discussions.

That data is being used to further curate the environment of your show. It shapes the news we are exposed to, directs how we are marketed to, and informs many of our policy decisions. The data about what we are letting into our environment not only matters, but it is creating our future experiences.

I used to think that topics I engaged with and cared about only impacted my life. Now I realize that now more than ever, my emotional capacity is visible and measurable in many ways. The choice to anchor our environment in our spiritual beliefs has an impact on the world around us. Your character has the power to shape what the human experience is becoming simply by expanding their environment and engaging differently.

I realize we cannot pay attention and care about every issue in the world, but we can choose to expand our environment over staying in a bubble.

That Chicago article perfectly illustrates how a horrific loss of life can become just a minor news story that reinforces the idea that some lives matter more than others. It reinforces the idea that some problems deserve solutions and others are hopeless. Is that the show we want to create?

Whether or not people pay attention to an issue has a dramatic effect on the resources and public support given to finding a solution. Our small acts that broaden our environment matter. For your show, they direct attention to short-term and long-term solutions. For your character, they may be the start of missions you deeply care about.

How we find our voice on topics and engage in service missions will look different for each of us. I am not an extrovert or a lover of social media. I engage when I can, but it is not authentic to my personality to be the loudest voice in a crowd. If you're like me, what we can do is read the article (even the long one). What we can do is struggle with the topics personally, so we have an informed point of view in the one-on-one conversations that come more naturally to us.

I know that, at times, I am so moved that I have to share things publicly or engage in ways that are well outside my comfort zone. I take notice of those signs that these problems move me with greater intensity. These signs have been and will continue to be guiding lights for me, as I pursue my life's work. They tell me what motivates me to action the most. Hold that thought as we will come back to it as we seek to hear our callings.

It is a struggle to set your show in the broader world. It is hard to resist living in a bubble when it is so comfortable and stretching our capacity is so hard.

Yet, your character knows that your show is not set in a bubble. Your character looks at the script we wrote in Part I and decides to act in a manner that engages deeply with life.

I write this knowing that I have been guilty of closing my emotional doors to the plight of strangers, those with differing viewpoints, "bad" people, sad current events, or problems that seem unsolvable. It was my go-to defense mechanism when I was already working so hard on trying to be happy in my own life. I *wasn't* anchored in my beliefs at that time nor feeling whole enough to be a part of God's work. My focus on comfort and validation was all-consuming at that point in my life.

Once your character knows they are whole and worthy of doing important work, they have a greater ability to engage in and see what the world needs from them. They have the ability to see what kind of problems they want to use their lives to work on solving.

YOUR CHOICE: TO GROW YOUR EXPERIENCES

You are reading this book because you want to take your spiritual beliefs and manifest the work your life was meant to produce. That desire is a necessary part of the process, but it is difficult to know how to convert that desire into actionable steps. How do you find your work callings, when you don't know where to start?

The first step (in the last chapter) is to spend time in your spiritual practice connecting with your spiritual being which strengthens your ability to listen to what your soul is telling you. The next step is to immerse yourself more deeply in the life experiences happening around you. This raises your awareness to the things you feel strongly about, which often leads to greater and more effortless motivation to work on these issues.

Ask yourself, what are you "feeling" right now? Can you easily tell?

Without practicing tuning into your feelings, it can be hard to pinpoint exactly how you feel. Happy? Sad? Bored? Some mix of all three?

Children instinctively know how they feel. Almost as soon as they learn about emotions, toddlers are letting us know "that makes me sad" or "that makes me happy." Years of being an adult tends to disconnect us from our feelings. We learn to avoid them with busyness and suppress them with vices. We notice only when we have reached complete exhaustion or fury, but feeling slightly tired, disrespected, or disappointed is much harder to notice. Yet, it is there driving our behavior whether we notice it or not.

Caring about the life experience outside of your daily bubble helps you get reacquainted and stay connected to your feelings. For example, are you familiar with your desire to be comforted? What about your version of low-lying fear? Are you familiar with how these things are triggered in you and how you experience these emotions in your mind, in your body, and in your soul?

We cannot think through the answers to questions of emotion. We have to feel them ourselves. Caring about the needs in the world gives us a chance to experience these feelings in a controlled environment. When we let ourselves feel the experience of others, we build our ability to assess our own emotions. We also strengthen the muscle that can tolerate emotional discomfort and vulnerability.

Letting in the range of emotions that come with the human experience takes work on our part. Living in a bubble is much easier, but it comes at the cost of our potential.

If we want to do daring work and build strong relationships in life, we need to be comfortable with vulnerability. When we live fully in our beliefs, vulnerability is something we will get to practice in each and every episode. We are trying to understand humanity better through connection. We are trying to grant others the best shot of fulfilling their own human potential through love. We are trying to break our own need for attachment for the sake of growth and fulfillment.

We build our tolerance to vulnerability every time we chose to care about anything or anyone we cannot control. Start with seeking out information that you wouldn't stumble upon on your own. Start by seeking to anchor your environment in the setting of the broader human experience—beyond your social-economic, cultural, or geographic bubble.

When anchored in our environment, we choose to read the news story that might make us feel disturbed or complicit. We seek to understand the emotions and life circumstances of the people we disagree with politically. We seek out and find people from diverse backgrounds (racial, social, religious, etc.) to engage with if daily surroundings don't bring them into our bubble.

EXERCISE

Next time you come across a tragic news story about a community you can't easily relate to, pause and try to feel yourself caring for the individuals involved in the story.

Imagine if it was you or someone you love. Let their faces stay in your mind. Let them in emotionally, fully knowing that you cannot fix things and probably won't see a way to immediately help them. Let that vulnerability in anyway.

Feel your feelings and your lack of control. Care about the human beings with souls that are no greater and no lesser than you despite their troubled circumstances.

CAPACITY AND COMPASSION

As I went through this experience, I learned that I had built up walls to caring about people I couldn't easily relate to. I would read the news story but immediately let my fears focus on why this situation was less likely to happen to me. In order to provide myself with that emotional assurance, I had to identify what the victim could and should have done differently. I had to blame the sufferer on some level, so I didn't feel that the same could happen to me or others I loved. I *wasn't* able to feel compassion for the beautiful souls of others and it took time to let those feelings in. I wanted to be compassionate, but wanting to care will not make you care on its own. It is something we have to practice. We have to identify our own barriers and grow a capacity for vulnerability.

We are not meant to act on everything we care about. Our work callings can't address every problem in the world. But through caring more, we receive data on what the world needs and what we care most about fixing. Consider it a fact-finding mission to see what pulls at your heart the most. To do that you have to care often and broadly and educate yourself as much as you can about the human experience.

Every time you do, you will get stronger and more comfortable with caring and accepting vulnerability. This will serve you when being vulnerable has higher personal stakes. It will make you better prepared to make life and work decisions that require you choose between the risk of stretching and growing or playing it safe and staying the same. That is what is in it for us. We get stronger spiritually and emotionally.

For our work, we are able to find meaning and passions from this data. What we are seeking is something we are deeply motivated to do. And there are so many ways that we can play a part in making the life experience of others better.

GROWING MORE HUMAN EXPERIENCES

When I think about doing good in the world it brings to mind Mother Nature's process of growing life around us through plants and flowers. Think of the seeds we might plant and the better human experience we hope to grow. And we can all play our part.

In farming, there are many tasks that lead to the harvest. Some focus on preparing the soil where seeds can flourish. Others focus on planting the seeds themselves. Some tasks include weeding because weeds have the potential to stymie our plants' growth. Someone has to monitor seedlings and ensure they are getting enough water or other nutrients. Someone does the work of collecting and using the harvest. They even collect seeds from one harvest to plant the next batch of crops. Each one of these jobs is important. The seed planter would be foolish to think preparing the soil doesn't matter as much. The person collecting the harvest would be wise to feel gratitude for the person that worked to rid the soil of weeds.

Your life's work will be unique to your passions and the space you are meant to impact. For example, the person that creates a work of art prepares the soil of humanity to experience the astounding beauty of what a single human life can create. Their art helps us get in touch with something spiritual that logic cannot adequately explain. The artist prepares the soil of humanity to be aware of the value of life, which prepares it for seeds of equality. We can all find our unique place and space to positively impact our show with our work.

No contributions are more valuable than another. What matters is that we engage genuinely. We will not all be on the front line as "seed planters" or "weed fighters," which are most publicly linked to service work. Those people often work at nonprofits, provide direct services, or fight for environmental or social justice. We need their roles greatly and have to support them, if we are not called to that kind of work. However, we will all be playing critical roles in advancing the life experience of others.

Are you open to engaging deeply with the world around you? Is there diversity in your experiences and relationships or could you do more to broaden your perspective? Is your heart open to the experience of others? Are you in touch with how you feel in general and what you care most about addressing in the human experience?

Work in the service of others will always point us to our happiest and most fulfilling tasks. Anchoring our environment to our beliefs is the path to finding and following our work callings. Our beliefs will lead us to respect our obligation to life, especially humanity, and reveal which problems we want to work on.

CHAPTER 11

AWARENESS

Our lives are made up of many moments strung together which tell the unique story of our existence. Awareness dictates how we perceive and experience each of these sacred moments. When we are aware, we work mindfully—embracing the precious opportunities inherent in every minute we are alive.

TIME AWARENESS

"What do you do?" This has to be one of the most common questions asked at cocktail parties and networking events. Many people select their career and take new work assignments with the subconscious goal of answering this question comfortably when called upon to do so.

"What do you do?"

"Oh, I'm an attorney" or "I'm a teacher" or "I'm a vice president for a medical device company."

I won't deny this question creates some social pressure. We know we will find ourselves at times needing to answer it and prefer when our answer makes it easier to be socially accepted or even grants us some social currency.

"I own a media business that works with (*fill in the blank celebrity*)" or "I am the CEO of XYZ software company."

Impressive or interesting titles do indeed engage people in social gatherings. But how much of our lives are spent at cocktail parties versus regular work days? How many hours do we spend *telling someone what we do* versus *doing what we do*?

In the last chapter, we explored our environment and challenged ourselves to stay engaged in the world. This chapter centers on being aware of how we use our time. We won't delve into time management, but rather time awareness.

THE QUESTION: AWARENESS OF LIFE'S BEAUTY

We have all heard the expression, "youth is wasted on the young." There is something about the phrase that everyone can relate to. No matter how old you are, there is likely a time in your life that you would enjoy and appreciate being able to live as your older self.

Even a child in middle school can appreciate that the classes were easier and playtimes more frequent in elementary school. I failed to appreciate the time in my life when I was free from paying bills and someone else cooked my meals. I can only imagine how nice it would be to have naptime back during my work days.

As we grow older there are more and more examples where we can see the value of a time that has passed. It is not that we long to relive the moments of our past, but simply that we would appreciate them differently if we had the benefit of knowing that they would end and never return again. Our youth *wasn't* wasted by our younger self, but it would be more fully appreciated by our older selves.

When we anchor our awareness in our spiritual beliefs, we see life's beauty as it is in the present moment. We place more value on our time while we are actually living it. To anchor our awareness in our beliefs is to be spiritually awake and open to what *is* happening, instead of what *was* happening, what *could* happen, what *should* happen, or what we *hope* will happen.

Anchoring our awareness in our spiritual beliefs gives us the gift of knowing how precious our time on this earth is. We also live our lives in a heightened sense of gratitude and eagerness to take advantage of opportunities. It opens us up to appreciating or seeing the paths to fulfillment that may be right in front of us. It also stops us from accepting a work existence that drains us most days but impresses other people when we happen to be at a cocktail party.

So, our question for this chapter follows the same format as the others. You will be asking yourself and ultimately answering:

Q: Is my awareness anchored in my beliefs?

ACCEPTING CHANGE

Change is an inevitable part of life and we can't escape that fact. Sometimes those changes are for the better and sometimes for the worse, but then it will change again. My mother always said, "This too shall pass," when things got hard in our lives to remind us that our painful seasons wouldn't last forever. Yet, the same applies when thinking about the happy seasons of our lives. The circumstances that made us happy will also pass. Change is simply a natural part of time.

It is always hard to let go of things, but especially when we have regrets. Often our regret is that we never fully appreciated what we had when we had it. That is not to say we didn't value it, but only that in hindsight we would have paid greater attention and valued it more. We may have done or said other things if we'd known how our remaining time was limited and precious.

When we have the opportunity to say goodbye to someone or something, we have at least those few precious moments to experience life with full awareness of time. If you have ever sat in a hospital room and said goodbye to someone you love, then you know exactly what I mean.

It applies to other situations in life as well. It could be those last few months at a job you loved before retirement. The last weeks at a company you founded before selling it. The last days in a city that changed your life before moving, the last summer before your child moved out, or putting on lotion before undergoing a surgery that will leave your body forever changed. When we clearly see change coming, we have greater awareness of how precious and temporary the time we have left is.

It is emotional to realize when we are running out of time. Yet, when we are fully aware of the precious nature of our time each moment is cherished and becomes sacred.

Living with the awareness that our time is sacred anchors life in our spiritual beliefs. Unfortunately, we usually fail to notice how precious a moment is, until it is obvious that change is imminent or a longing for a past moment has emerged. That doesn't mean that the time was any less precious while we were living it, but only that we failed to notice.

Failing to notice the sacred quality of time limits our opportunity to experience the exquisite joy of being alive. Seeing a loved one in the hospital just before death is not the same as having a chance to fully appreciate a laugh with them over a routine lunch years prior. Cherishing the final days before selling a business is not the same experience as appreciating the gift of holding each of the routine staff meetings along the way.

It is a blessing to have moments of full awareness prior to a change. It helps us transition and say goodbye. Yet, it is a missed opportunity to let the many frequent and routine moments of our lives pass by without appreciating the miraculous gift we have.

I used to think of mindfulness as a state of calm or serenity. I now view it as a practice of focusing my attention on the value of my life experience. I ask myself: Am I aware of what is happening around me in the present moment or am I lost in thought about the past or the future? Am I forgetting just how precious this moment is and may be to me someday? Will there be a time in my life when I long to experience something (big or small) that I am failing to appreciate right now? Am I directing my senses to fully see, hear, smell, and touch all that I can experience? Mindfulness directs me to remember that my time is a sacred gift.

Working whole is mindful working and requires that we show up in our lives prepared to fully experience all that we can do, see, and be.

YOUR TIME

A combination of the show's setting and time help your actor orient to their character's life. The actor's work is to interpret how your character would behave in response to those factors.

Your show is set in the world outside your personal bubble, but your character is going to occupy concrete spaces on a day-to-day basis, such as their home or workplace. Likewise, your show is set across all of time, but your character is going to occupy a finite space that is clearly defined by your lifespan. How should you be thinking about the role time plays?

Acting out your script also requires that you put your character's lifespan into the context of all of history since the beginning and running to the end of time. I cannot comprehend when time might have started or consider when it might end. What I know for sure is that our lives are exceptionally short in comparison.

Your character will only appear in a few seasons of the show and then they will be gone. That is the reality that your actor should reflect on. Your actor will have to be aware that they are here to add a new dimension to the show in the time they will be participating, but they can never forget how short and precious their time in front of the camera will be.

In the show anchored in our beliefs each moment is our one and only opportunity to experience life and evolve your character. Tomorrow we will not be who we are today. When we go to bed at night we are saying goodbye to a day that can never be relived. Yet, we wake every morning to a new day that will welcome, challenge, and change us a little more. Time is a miraculous idea.

We are going to focus our episodes on the days of our lives because Mother Nature seems to have chosen days as a cycle of importance. The sun rises and falls daily (in most places) and our bodies seem to follow that cycle as well. We don't rest once a week, month, or year. We rest once a day and that makes a day the perfect time frame to focus our attention on. Within your day lies a finite amount of time for work and for rest. What do you want to do with it?

Remember Freytag's pyramid in Chapter 2. Within each episode the writers have chosen to orient the show with a start in gratitude (exposition), a goal to increase connection (rising action), a conflict that requires growth from your character (climax), the power to live in truth (falling action), and the patience to wait for the seasons of life to unfold (dénouement).

LIVING EACH DAY IN TIME

When we reflect on the fact that each script is set in a single day, we are able to release a lot of the stress that comes from living for the future. We are able to live only that one day with the intention of maximizing our life experience and our spiritual growth. When the actor considers what time the show is set in, the answer is always "the present moment." Your character's scenes are set in the only time period we can ever impact in the show.

I rarely stop to do exercises while reading a book. I read the description of them and briefly pause to think about the purpose, but then continue reading. I assume some of you are doing the same with the ones in this book. However, if at all possible make the time to do the following exercise.

EXERCISE

Open a new page in your journal and for the next few days, or weeks, I'd like you to carry it with you so that you can capture a list throughout the day.

The first step is to set aside at least 30 minutes to start writing down the names of people that have used their time to impact your life in some way. Consider this list to be your own version of the Emmys. If you were giving out awards to actors that have delivered outstanding performances in your show, who would you give your awards to? Luckily, we don't have to pick the "best" contribution nor limit ourselves to categories. We will be acknowledging everyone that has had an impact.

Don't limit your list to famous or "great" people or people that you care most about. Focus your attention on the contributions more than how you feel about the person. Who has used their time to add to your enjoyment, growth, or well-being?

There will be many names that come to you immediately. That is what that first step is meant to capture. Try to flush it out as fully as you can so you can move on to the next step. Add parents, teachers, friends, and colleagues that made a difference or inspired you in some way. There is no one too minor to capture, even if a small action had an impact on you.

The first list alone will be long. Carry that list with you for a few days and keep adding anyone that comes to mind as a new addition. Bosses you had several jobs ago, coworkers that kept you sane, financial professionals that helped you start a business or attend college. Don't stop until you think you have covered almost everyone you can come up with. A sign that you are ready to move to the next step is when you are no longer able to add proper names, but instead are adding descriptors like "that lunch lady from third grade" or "the person that let me into traffic yesterday."

Finally, start listing those people that have impacted you from a distance. It is likely that you have never, and will never, meet these people. The list is unique to what matters to you, but some examples are:

- Producers, writers, and actors of shows, movies, or plays, you've enjoyed.

- The CEO, creative director, or supply chain manager of a company whose products make your life better or easier.

- The authors of books that have shaped your thinking.

- The publishers of books that have helped you grow.

- Artists that have inspired you.

- Comedians that make you laugh.

- Service providers that bring you comfort or enable your lifestyle.

- The builder, architect, or engineer that created the home you live in.

- Inventors and technologists that made something unimaginable part of your reality.

- Creators of governmental or work policies you benefit from.

- Administrators of services of functions you need.

- Medical providers that help maintain or heal your body.

- Medical providers that saved the life of someone you love.

- Musicians, writers, and poets that help you connect to, understand, and process your emotions.

- Clothing designers or beauty professionals that help you connect with the exquisite nature of your physical self.

- A current or historical person that is using/ used their lives to protect you or grant you freedoms.

- Religious figures that illuminate your spiritual path.

- Farmers that bring nourishment.

- Chefs that create culinary art with God's creations.

This list could go on and on, but I hope you get the idea. The purpose of the exercise is to try to wrap your brain around the volume of people and the variety of ways that others' time can impact your show.

You may think that you can conceptualize this idea without doing the exercise. You may think that just from reading the list above you have the gist of what it will reveal to you. Please do not stop with just thinking about this exercise—actually do it. The magic comes from the experience of noticing the magnitude of people that matter to you personally and in your show.

An example from my own list is a parking attendant at a hotel in Washington, D.C. where I had an important job interview scheduled. If you know D.C., you know we are known for our traffic. It is not as bad as New York or Los Angeles, but we usually rank #3 for worst traffic in the United States. On this particular day, I allowed two full hours to travel 30 miles, but it still wasn't enough. I can remember sweating and praying as it became clear to me that I might be late.

When I pulled into the valet of the hotel with two minutes to spare, the parking attendant informed me that the hotel parking garage was reserved for guests only and not for those eating in the restaurant. I started to beg. I explained that I was there for a job interview and he offered me a moment of grace. He parked my car for no charge (clearly, I gave him a large tip afterwards) in front of the building until I returned.

I got the job and I think of him often to this day. I wonder how it might have turned out had I been late to the interview. I think about how he has no idea what that job has meant to my life's work. He's likely forgotten all about me. I will probably never see him again and I don't know his name, but he will forever be on my list.

Your list could go on for the rest of your life. I continue to add to mine every chance I get. Once you get started, you may want to keep doing it for a long time. It helps to put into perspective how many degrees of separation there can be between a person living their own episodes and the impact they can have on the overall show.

What all the people on your list will have in common is how they used their time. Each person used a moment (or many moments) to do work that impacted you. They could not have predicted while doing the work exactly how or how much you might be impacted. There is a good chance that even now they have no idea that you specifically value the work of their lives. They simply showed up and did their work in the present moment, but the impact of it was and will always be out of their hands. Impact comes in the future. Life is lived in the present.

This is why knowing "what time it is" shapes our lives. It encourages us to surrender the outcomes of our work to God. Meanwhile we get to bask in the glory of the present moment and the joy of simply doing what we feel called to. There is no pressure to achieve or chase after certain future outcomes, but we find fulfillment in our present experience.

Businesses, careers, books, plays, works of art, and nonprofits are not built in the future, but are manifested from many actions and opportunities taken in present moments. We have to be oriented to maximizing the value of our time.

Use your time with the acknowledgment that it is sacred because it will orient you toward seeing opportunities and taking action.

That is what it means to know the time in your show. Your character doesn't take for granted that their role is temporary. Your character doesn't forget that their time in front of the camera is limited and precious, so you're always looking for opportunities to appreciate and impact the show.

YOUR CHOICE:
TO SPEND YOUR TIME MINDFULLY

"How do you spend your time?"

This is the question I'd like to hear asked more often of people at cocktail parties. This question is not about our titles; it is about our lives. What are we doing with our time? What does it say about the life we are living?

We pick up spiritual lessons from a variety of places, but one that has stayed in my mind is from a religious service I attended several years ago. I don't remember what the sermon entailed, but I know that the climax of the message included the pastor saying, "Go to sleep in peace. Wake up in joy."

Over the years, I have thought about this phrase frequently. I know instinctively that the measure of how well my life is anchored to my spiritual beliefs is whether I can do just these two simple things—go to sleep in peace and wake up in joy. Sometimes when I lie in bed at night I say the phrase to myself over and over. I take an account of whether my day was anchored in the truth of this phrase. How did I spend my time today? Was I joyful? Am I now at peace? No matter the answer, I hope that I plant a seed in my spirit to wake up with joy the next morning.

Our days, perhaps especially our routine days, are the very fruit of our lives. They are the product of the decisions we have made. Our experience today is a result of how we have valued and directed our time on this earth to date. Did we choose the bolder path or the safer one? Did we choose to be challenged or comfortable? Did we choose the invigorating, the more interesting, or the more authentic experience?

If you would be saddened, bored, overwhelmed, or embarrassed to tell a stranger your honest answer to how you spend your time, it is not too late to choose a different path and experience your precious life with the sacred brilliance that it deserves. I don't mean that your days have to be filled with amusement parks and celebrity sightings. That isn't what makes us go to sleep in peace or wake up in joy.

Instead I'm encouraging you to anchor your awareness in your spiritual beliefs. To be aware of how precious and temporary our entire life experience is (even the routine moments). We change diapers with our time. We clean our bathrooms with our time. We cook yet another Wednesday dinner, attend one more work meeting, and send another email. And in it all, there we are alive. Getting another chance to experience our lifetime. There we are often failing to notice how even the very next moment is not promised and how unpredictable future circumstances may be.

The time to live fulfilled is right now. Here in the present moment is the only time we can chart our course and experience the fullness of our lives. Your work callings will be heard, followed, take shape, and manifest all in single moments spread across many days. We have to have the motivation and stamina to value the experience of our time alive enough to stay engaged in the work we are called to do.

Our awareness of the value of time helps us to decide what we show up for and what we don't. Are we shedding toxic relationships because we can't possibly spare our sacred time on them? Are we engaging in the activities that give us energy and joy because we can't possibly miss our sacred time to do so? Are we cooking that routine meal with the joy and wonder of the time we have in this life to be physically and mentally competent enough to perform the task? These are all questions of time and there are many more. But they all lead us back to our ability to go to sleep in peace and wake up in joy.

The next chapter is about our wants and desires, and is perhaps my favorite chapter, but don't rush to get there. This question is a big one and the time you will devote to work hinges on your awareness of the sacred gift of each moment.

CHAPTER 12

PRIORITIES

Our priorities reveal what is most important to us and influence how we pursue getting what we want. When our highest priority is to seek spiritual growth, we will consistently direct our work lives toward the choices that lead us to fulfillment.

HAVING IT ALL

At the very beginning of a job search, I work with clients to clarify their priorities. We want a lot of things from our work, but some things are more important than others depending on our life stage. Some of my clients cannot relocate or need to reduce their travel time, and that has implications on the opportunities they can pursue. Some are seeking a particular title or type of challenge and are willing to compromise on everything else from job location to compensation. Some of the easiest clients to help are those that share with me that making more money (or the most they can) is their top priority. That immediately focuses their search toward certain roles and company types.

The key to pursuing a process that will meet their desires is that clients need to be honest with me. I need them to tell me that money is important and not worry that I will think they are shallow or greedy. I need them to tell me that working less so they can spend time at home with family (or simply because they are tired) is most important and not worry that I'll think they are lazy or not as motivated as others. I harbor no judgment in my clients' priorities. Each desire is valid. What I need is the clarity around the true importance, so I can counsel them toward meeting that goal with the appropriate level of focus.

We desire many things from our work, but it seems almost impossible at times to "have it all."

- We want to earn enough to comfortably pay our bills and have enough left over for savings, leisure, and luxuries.

- We want to feel secure financially without having to trade away our quality of life.

- We want to get up on a Monday morning and actually look forward to going to work.

- We want to grow and feel useful while we are alive and be remembered for having mattered when we are gone.

We want all these things from our professional lives, yet it feels as if having one of these dreams fulfilled requires trading away another. If we want to be financially secure, do we have to trade our ability to enjoy the work we do? If we want to produce something worthwhile, do we have to give up having enough time to enjoy other parts of our lives? These are real paradoxes in the human world of work.

This book, however, is not for people seeking to anchor their lives in the human reality, but those seeking to make sense of the role their spiritual beliefs can and should play in their work lives.

THE QUESTION: PRIORITIES— RECONCILING TWO WORLDS

Almost all spiritual traditions assume that the spiritual believer will have to learn to live in two worlds simultaneously. In the spiritual world, we are told to believe that God, or the universe, will provide what we actually need. We are challenged to live in contentment and gratitude with whatever we have.

In the human world, we are told to strive to make more money, so we can provide the things we need and the things we want. The line is often blurred between these two categories, making it hard to decide what is a "need" versus a "want." We need clothes, homes, and transportation. We need to plan for our retirements and buy life insurance. But how much is enough? When do we cross the line between meeting a need and pursuing a want?

It is hard to reconcile these two worlds, especially when it is so difficult to know what our needs are. We wonder if anchoring in the spiritual world will ever be enough to meet our human desires. And we fear that prioritizing our spiritual goals will require unrealistic trade-offs in the human world.

I hope you have been asking yourself if your identity, environment, and awareness are anchored in your spiritual beliefs. Now we will be deciding on our priorities. What do you want more than anything else? Is it really spiritual growth? Is your life goal to live in fulfillment or do you want to prioritize comfort, achievement, or accumulation?

As you move through this chapter, ask yourself:

Q: Are my priorities anchored in my beliefs?

In the Christian faith, there is a song called *Amazing Grace*. This song is likely one of the most famous spirituals ever written. The lines that stick out in my mind are:

> Amazing grace, how sweet the sound
> that saved a wretch like me
> I once was lost, but now I'm found
> Was blind but now I see.

This highlights a key part of all spiritual journeys—the awakening to, or rebirth in, the spiritual world. This is how we first arrived on whatever spiritual path we chose. The first step was to see the spiritual world as a way out of the fog of lonely and meaningless suffering. *Amazing Grace* is about the unfathomable gifts this first step of the spiritual journey provides—redemption and hope. Finding redemption and hope can set us free from unworthiness and get us going in a new direction toward fulfillment. From there we are tasked with using our spiritual path to transform our human lives.

If your story is anything like mine, it took an enormous amount of effort to simply awaken spiritually. I showed up to the starting line bruised and weary, and needing a place to rest before I could go anywhere else. I have since learned that my experience is not uncommon. I was "lost" and then I was "found," but I didn't yet have the strength to start walking on my spiritual path. I got stuck for a good long while sitting at the starting line—aware of the path, but not following it. I kept waiting for more spiritual growth to happen and my daily life to transform without putting in the sustained effort needed to walk the path that leads to it.

Finding the path is certainly the start of the journey but following and staying on the path leads to more significant opportunities for growth. Along our spiritual journey, there are many spiritual classrooms where we can learn how to anchor what we believe and transform our lives. The classroom of work is a major one, but there are many others. At some point, you may also be called to the classroom of marriage and the classrooms of parenthood, grief, caretaking, or friendship.

When our priorities are anchored to our spiritual beliefs, we walk into the classroom of work with courage and sit there long enough to soak in the lessons it has to teach us. Work (similar to parenthood or grief) is one of the more effective spiritual classrooms. It is more effective only because we have little choice about being in the classroom. Most people stick out parenthood or sit with their grief no matter what. And thanks to our need for money and financial security, most of us stay in the classroom of work, even when we are not actively learning anything. While other, equally important, spiritual classrooms like marriage, friendship, or caretaking are more easily abandoned. We feel freer to leave those classrooms entirely when learning the lessons there becomes too hard or no longer helpful to us.

The classroom of work similar to all others has the potential to teach us our essential spiritual lessons if we allow it to. The work lessons of our lives are where we can find a place of spiritual study, spiritual practice, and it is certainly where our beliefs will be tested.

The question this chapter asks us to explore is whether our highest priority in life is truly living fulfilled and how can our work decisions help us get there. Is that what you want more than anything else? Because if so, you will embrace the lessons that your character would be motivated to learn in the classroom of work.

YOUR MOTIVATION

In the last three chapters, we analyzed what it will mean to play your character according to your script. Your character is whole and worthy, so you don't need to affirm your identity from outside accomplishments. Instead, you are seeking to discern what you can contribute uniquely to the overall story of life. You are aware that your time is sacred and plan to live each day with meaning.

You now know many things about your show and character. Yet, we haven't explored what your character truly wants and how it impacts your work. For an actor, this is called a character's "primary motivation." It is the underlying driver for everything they do. All actions on stage will be executed with the goal of getting what your character wants.

We are likely to follow several work callings over the course of our lives. The decisions we make about how we use our time and gifts mark out many of the conflicts we experience. However, there is a larger and more important yearning that longs to be fulfilled: the desire to integrate our spiritual path with our human life. We want to use our beliefs to fully realize peaceful, joyful, and resilient living—not in the afterlife, but here and now.

Part I grounds the kind of show that your character is choosing to live in. It focuses on your spiritual beliefs first, but also explores where those beliefs may impact your work. Our spiritual path is what leads us to a life of fulfillment. Following that path is what matters most.

Manifesting the kind of spiritual growth that transforms your human experience is your character's primary motivation. To do that, your character has to see each and every life experience as part of their spiritual learning process. And there are many spiritual lessons that work can teach us if we allow it to, but the three main ones are:

- How to get and stay in dialogue with God.
- How to be at peace with uncertainty.
- How to embrace change.

Each lesson presents a unique opportunity for your character to not only deepen their understanding of the beliefs we covered in Part I, but also to move those beliefs from ideas in the spiritual world to actions manifested in the human one. This is what your character wants.

WORK LESSONS

Let's explore each lesson and how your character can choose to practice it.

WORK LESSON #1:
GET AND STAY IN A DIALOGUE WITH GOD

Work callings can start with a tiny whisper from our soul. They come from a desire to discover our gifts and live as the person we are uniquely called to be. These whispers are the first reminder that we can live in dialogue with God (or the spiritual world, if that term resonates more).

I am guilty of ignoring many of my own work whispers. They came to me as daydreams of a different work life or an interesting yet seemingly unachievable idea. I either ignored them completely or told myself that they were impractical if not impossible. Maybe you have done the same. We often hear subtle callings toward our next work endeavor, but it is difficult to know if we should move forward and how to get started. Perhaps you've had a passing desire to own a business, start a nonprofit, write a book, build an online community, create a product, or pursue a new field of study.

A bold work calling gives us a reason to start and stay in dialogue with God. Listening for direction opens our eyes to the many ways that God might speak to and through us. This helps us live in the power of the spiritual world while we are tasked to work in the human one.

Following a work calling from a dream or idea to a realized vision is like navigating in the dark with a flashlight. You can only see a few feet in front of you, but you trust that it will light the way as you continue to step forward. Whenever you need more direction you will have only one place to turn—back to God.

WORK LESSON #2:
BE AT PEACE WITH UNCERTAINTY

In the last chapter, we dealt with the uncertainty of time. Not only can we not predict what time will bring, but we cannot control when change will occur. Our beliefs are there to help us be at peace with uncertainty and therefore relish the value of the present moment.

The classroom of work offers ample practice and test after test on our ability to embrace uncertainty. If our life's callings were clearly defined, step-by-step, and devoid of risk, we would not need to be called to them. We would not need love to learn to listen for them nor power to manifest them. The very nature of work callings is daring and unpredictable.

Our body of work is revealed one work calling at a time. We embark on a lifelong journey to keep exploring and discovering what our soul is capable of throughout our life's appearance in the show.

The term "calling" is often used to represent the idea that a life can and should have one singular work mission. We talk about a calling as a specific gift a person should go out and identify, and perhaps feel inferior or unmotivated when we are unable to pinpoint exactly what our life's single calling should be.

Your character doesn't see it this way. Instead they understand that the purpose of work is to serve their primary motivation to grow and live their fullest life experience, and their legacy is all those small deposits of good, while learning how to anchor life's priorities in the spiritual world. Your character knows this is the only goal worth pursuing.

In the classroom of work, we are challenged to accept the uncertainty of not knowing where the work is going to take us or what impact it will have. We are tested on our ability to accept uncertainty and take the journey anyway. If we want to follow work callings we face uncertainty at every turn, from discerning early whispers to knowing when one calling has ended and it is time to start another. Every step along the way must be made despite uncertainty, but peace comes when we learn to embrace the spiritual process and simply enjoy the journey.

Surrendering the illusion of control and enjoying the journey in all areas of our lives is what will lead us to enduring joy and fulfillment. We can learn lessons on how to do it in a variety of places, but the classroom of work is happy to provide pop quizzes and tests on how we are doing. The point is to stay in the classroom, get our work done, and keep learning the lessons.

WORK LESSON #3:
EMBRACE CHANGE

The last lesson was about accepting the things we cannot control, but the classroom of work also teaches us how to change the things we should not accept. In the words of Reinhold Niebuhr:

God, grant me the serenity to accept the things I cannot change,

The courage to change the things I can,

And the wisdom to know the difference.

There are hardships in life that we get little choice in having to bear. The ones that come to mind immediately are trauma, health issues, family dynamics, and grief. When it comes to our work lives, we have to accept that we cannot know in advance what our body of work will be. We have to accept that there will be some purposes we will be called to and others we will not. Accepting is a skill the classroom of work demands we practice.

However, this work lesson teaches us how to implement change. There are many things that are out of our control, but much of our daily experience is shaped by the things we do and do not do. The classroom of work tests our ability to make the changes that align with our beliefs.

Fully bloomed flowers do not look at all like the seeds they sprouted from and have to adjust to life above the surface. Anything that grows must change.

Work callings tend to change the direction of our lives. They tend to require capabilities from us that we do not have yet, or do not know we have. We have to embrace change to follow a work calling. Your character wants to live each episode growing and living authentically. Your character doesn't want to have a daily existence in the human world that is separated from a spiritual path. Yet that is exactly the place that most of us start our spiritual journeys. We were asleep before we awakened to the spiritual path. We were likely living an everyday existence that was driven by self-soothing and distraction. To follow the spiritual path and grow requires significant change.

For example, in the process of writing this book I have had to grow from not having enough time to work on a passion project to changing my life to make the time. I had to be honest about my priorities, so I could make space for writing. It necessitated some uncomfortable discussions with people I cared about. It meant not showing up at things I used to attend and having to deal with others, knowing I had changed focus (possibly in a way they didn't like). There was no way to fully maintain my old life without stifling my spiritual growth and the possibilities for my work. Embracing difficult, yet necessary, changes is unavoidable, if the primary motivation is to anchor our priorities in our spiritual beliefs.

EXERCISE

Take out your journal and spend some time reflecting on the spiritual lessons your work life may be trying to teach you.

- Where have you already experienced a spiritual work lesson?
- What value has it added into your life?

> · Which lesson are you most in need of learning right now—maintaining a dialogue with God, accepting uncertainty, or embracing change?

YOUR CHOICE:
TO OPEN A DIALOGUE

The biggest enemy of working whole is the separation of spirituality from our daily lives. It is easy to assign our spiritual work to places of worship, weekly rituals, or sacred holidays. That not only limits the amount of time we spend in pursuit of spiritual fulfillment, but also gives us a false notion of control over the human world and limits our growth. When we anchor our priorities in our spiritual beliefs we will pursue our work with different goals and motivations.

Are you manifesting your work in dialogue with God?

While pursuing my own work callings, I have received inspiration and direction in the most unexpected ways. I didn't hear the voice of God directly, but I learned to notice when thoughts drifted in seemly out of nowhere and refined my vision or plan of attack. I learned to acknowledge the coincidences that randomly made my path forward easier than I expected. I learned to marvel at the miracles appearing in my daily life, from the people that showed up with the missing piece of information to the opportunity that arrived precisely when I needed it most.

There were also many times when God told me to wait and be still. Just because I was asking for direction about next steps didn't mean I was told to move forward immediately. Yet, I thank God for the times he told me to wait and I did. Many blessings and better work outcomes have come from the lesson in patience. I thank him for the times he told me to wait and I did not. I learned a lot from those experiences as well. I learned to appreciate what it feels like to be at peace in my soul versus the stress of letting my ego tell me I can control the situation. All of these experiences in the classroom of work taught me how to live in a dialogue with the spiritual world.

The authentic work callings I have been able to pursue because of my dialogue with God is quite meaningful to me, but the spiritual relationship it has taught me how to build is much more valuable to my well-being. That is why the work remains a secondary priority. The spiritual growth is what will lead me to fulfillment not any achievement or success that work can deliver.

Are you at peace with the uncertainty of your life's work?

I wonder sometimes what my own body of work will be. Will I have a cohesive portfolio, or will it be a tapestry of seemly disjointed yet meaningful projects? The classroom of work will require that we be at peace with the uncertainty of not knowing what our impact may be and what is coming next.

Understanding your full body of work will not be possible until all your work callings have been heard and followed. Even after your death, your work will live on and could change direction and meaning. Like you, I'm also working to embrace the greater spiritual lesson that allows me to focus on the joy of living my life instead of trying to predict the outcomes of my work.

Are you using your work to embrace change?

The classroom of work has taught me how to use love as a way of making daily decisions on where I should be, who I should be with, and what I should be doing. But more importantly, it has given me the power to actually implement those decisions and change my life.

I know many people currently following their spiritual work callings to birth things like new businesses, new career paths, or community missions that are consciously sitting in the classroom of work learning to embrace change. Are you? Knowing we are in the classroom and choosing to practice, learn, and be tested is what matters. Surrendering to the classroom and accepting the tests is where the spiritual transformation occurs.

It is hard to be motivated to change for change's sake alone, but our work callings are driven from things we will find uniquely meaningful and fulfilling. The call to our unique work is embedded deep in our soul and has the power to push us to make changes we might otherwise avoid. The classroom of work can create the change because it requires we anchor our priorities to our spiritual beliefs and into our daily human lives.

Every day, we have to get up ready to embrace the lessons we will encounter in pursuit of our callings. When we fail to do so, we fail to produce our best work and live in the fulfillment we are seeking. Are you willing to practice in and be tested by the classroom of work?

As we leave this chapter, we have yet to explore some of the more practical elements of finding and pursuing a work calling. This has been intentional. We have to first learn to listen before we can be called. All the chapters so far have prepared us to open our hearts and minds to the spiritual lessons work seeks to teach us. Is learning those lessons what you want most? Is living in spiritual fulfillment what you pursue above any other human goal? If so, you are ready to get to work.

CHAPTER 13

ACTIONS

Our actions are all the things we do and say, usually in pursuit of a conscious or subconscious goal. Fulfillment can only be realized by aligning our top priorities to our daily activities. Actions are the driving force that bring our highest work into fruition.

STAYING ALIGNED

In the early phases of a job search, the first task is to gain clarity on a client's goals and priorities. This is usually an enjoyable exercise and leaves clients feeling focused and invigorated for the pursuit ahead. We spend time figuring out what they want from their next work experience and how they should go about pursuing it.

They gain clarity on the goals themselves, but perhaps more importantly, I provide a confirmation that someone else deems their goals as appropriate and worthy of pursuit. They want to know that their goals are daring enough because who wants to settle for less than their best? And they also want to know that I think it is possible to realize their vision based on what I have seen others do. From there, we come up with a plan to align their actions to their goals.

Yet once the search reaches the middle stages, many clients choose to broaden their search beyond their original goals. They go from focusing on roles that are a clear promotion to also being open to jobs that are similar to the one they previously had. An example of this is the Chief Operating Officer (COO) that is ready to be CEO, and yet starts to be open to considering other COO roles again. They come back to me several weeks or months into the search feeling wearier instead of invigorated and deciding it is better to "leave their options open."

The problem with this "leaving your options open" strategy is that it changes the focus of their actions. If the goal is to become CEO then it is not a good use of their time or energy to interview for other COO jobs. And frankly, if you are already a COO you are going to be presented with more opportunities to be a COO again than those willing to take a risk on you as a first-time CEO.

Finding and securing your first CEO position requires extensive networking and patience. They will have less time for those actions, if they are busy interviewing for other COO jobs *and* their emotions will be quite conflicted when they start gaining traction or even receive an offer to become COO yet again. The easier career step will usually develop faster and leave them with an agonizing decision to make: Should I take this job offer now or continue to wait it out?

It is amazing what people are willing to tell themselves when they are presented a safer opportunity. They forget all the early discussions around why they feel called to be CEO. Now, don't get me wrong, these COO jobs are great offers. It is a luxury to be able to turn such a thing down, but in accepting them they miss the opportunity to pursue what they really wanted in the first place.

Part of my job is trying to keep my clients' actions aligned with what they want. That leaves me encouraging patience and focus, but also having to address the client's vulnerability which is created by turning down good, safe opportunities that won't lead to their goals. It is exciting to decide which new doors to try to open but closing old ones can be scary.

THE QUESTION:
LEARNING TO ANCHOR OUR ACTIONS

Getting what we want from our work life is not a mental exercise, it has to be executed by our actions—the things we do, say, where we go, and who we are with. And it is also what we don't do, what we don't say, where we don't go, and who we don't spend time with. When our actions are not aligned with what we say we want most, we arrive at different outcomes. We often find ourselves slowly reverting back to the easier and less vulnerable path and ending up stuck in the same place we started.

In our spiritual lives, we know what we want. We want to achieve the kind of spiritual growth that will transform our daily existence. Now we need to anchor our actions in the human world to help us achieve this goal.

The classroom of work, which we explored in the previous chapter, can serve as a place where we learn to anchor our actions in our beliefs. It can be a place to practice building a dialogue with God, accepting the uncertainty inherent in life, and making the changes needed to live what we believe. These are the goals we have for our lives, not just our work. The classroom of work is merely a place where we can learn how to achieve these goals.

This chapter seeks to show you how to use your actions to lead you to your work and get what you want spiritually. Instead of viewing work as a mechanism to win security, praise, or status, we will be viewing work as a path to learning how to manifest the focused, fulfilling, and meaningful daily existence we desire most.

We are seeking to live in an environment where the growth and enjoyment of our spiritual life outweighs the fear of risk and desire to control the outcomes of our work.

When we anchor our actions with our beliefs, we use our time and gifts to increase our ability to listen and engage with the spiritual world to manifest our work. Throughout this chapter, ask yourself:

Q: Are my actions anchored in my beliefs?

A calling by definition means being summoned by someone or something. As we discussed in the last chapter, learning to listen for a calling requires that you get and stay in dialogue with the spiritual world. However you choose to describe your spiritual path, you are listening for a pull from the divine spirit within, the universe, or God. You are using that direction to decide where your actions should lead you to show up in life. Because whether we listen for our work callings or not, we will show up in certain places and do work.

Work itself is inevitable for those of us that need to make a living. At the end of our lives we will see the complete picture of the work our actions led us to. It will include a collection of many work experiences. All the creation of our actions. All pursued one at a time. Some of our work experiences we may have been called to and others we have stumbled on or directed ourselves to reach.

EXERCISE

Take out your journal and explore where you have chosen to show up already at this point in your life. These have been your work classrooms to date.

- What academic institutions did your actions lead you to?

- What jobs, community projects, or business ventures did your actions create?

- What networks have your actions developed?

- Did you choose to show up in these places because you prioritized the spiritual fulfillment that comes from being truly engaged in your sacred life or were your actions motivated by something else?

In the career where our actions are self-directed, calculated, and anchored in personal achievement, we experience varying degrees of enjoyment from our work. We force ourselves to do things we don't want to do in an effort to achieve goals that are not our highest priority. So the point of anchoring your actions in your beliefs is to pursue a goal that gives you lasting fulfillment and joy. It will require that you align your actions to the things that deliberately build the spiritual connection which calls you to your work.

YOUR TACTIC

In acting, there is something called a "character tactic." Through dialogue and actions, the character tries to influence the action to get what they want. If one tactic fails, they try a new one and keep at it until it works. Your character is striving to live a fulfilled life, and this motivates their actions in each scene. This is how your character answers the question: How will I get what I want?

The show has paved the way for your character to prioritize spiritual fulfillment over any achievement in the human world. We have used our beliefs to reduce the distractions and fears that would create other primary motivations. There is nothing your character wants more than the peace, contentment, joy, and resilience that will come from walking their spiritual path.

Getting on, staying on, and walking the path is the goal. It is all your character wants because it will lead to their most joyful life experience. Our work lives are a mechanism to help us learn to fully engage in our spiritual lives and show up for the work experiences we were uniquely meant to have.

While learning to be in dialogue with God, your character has to focus their actions on making time, and creating quiet space within them, to hear these subtle callings. This may sound like a spiritual endeavor but it is only achieved through the real-world actions of your character's tactics. Tactics such as:

ACTIONS

- Where are you spending your time and are your actions aligned with creating space for spiritual fulfillment? This can only happen if you are willing to do new things, but also stop doing some of your current things. Your character won't create more space for the work you are called to, if they are not willing to cut out anything they are currently doing.

- Are the words you use with yourself and others aligned with your spiritual priorities? Are you willing to stop using your words to glorify "money" and "success," and instead prioritize peace, service to others, joyful experiences, and rest?

- What are your daily spiritual rituals and are you prioritizing them over other chores or habits? Are your daily actions focused on manifesting a deeper connection with God? What is on your "to-do list" and how much of the list is focused on tasks that anchor you in the spiritual world?

- What or who is draining or distracting you and are your actions aligned with limiting that exposure? Are you seeking more of that which breeds fear or anxiety in your thoughts or less? This can be anything from news, to social media, to reality TV shows, to social interactions. None of these are inherently bad, but your character has to seek to understand to what extent they align with your goals and anchor your actions accordingly. Sometimes that may mean engaging more in these activities, but often it means engaging less. Your character seeks to be deliberate in anchoring your daily exposures to your highest priority.

- Are you seeking a joyful life experience? Are you finding ways to engage with the things that make you feel most alive? Are you laughing? Are you spending time noticing the beauty in nature? Are you making time to do the things you are passionate about and interested in?

When your character anchors your actions with what you believe, you are able to live in the show that your beliefs created.

Your show is a comedy—whimsical and humorous most of the time. Your character desires to live each day inspired and motivated. Your character is not here to play a role that simply endures meaningless labor. Your actions should lead you to daily activities that invigorate you spiritually. We shouldn't have to convince ourselves to get up in the morning and face our lives. The time we get to play a part in our show is too limited and precious to waste. Our work should be something we are deeply drawn to and enjoy.

LOVE WHAT YOU DO

Work is often seen as something we force into our lives. It may be hard to do our work at times, but it should never be without pleasure and amusement. A marker of following a work calling is that we feel intrinsically motivated to keep going. We are focused while doing our highest work and it brings us joy simply from the experience of it.

Whispers of passion are the starting point for our work callings. They point us in the direction of potential classrooms where we might learn the most. Before we can enter those classrooms, we must learn to listen to the whispers of desire and let them grow loud enough to call us somewhere. We also have to be willing to resist the fear of uncertainty so that we can ultimately show up in that classroom ready to learn.

If we are not specific about where we choose to show up, we risk pursuing work that doesn't mean enough to teach us the spiritual lessons we seek to learn. Without proper inspiration to do our work, day in and day out, we won't be motivated enough to seek God continuously for direction and take the risks that will test our beliefs. Work is most effective as a spiritual classroom when we have a true calling to it.

Listening for a work calling isn't the same as listening for the jobs we should hold or the business venture we should start next. A work calling is a project or experience we are pursuing rather than a title or accomplishment. A work calling is there to prioritize our time and build increasing enjoyment and meaning into each day.

Some work callings lead immediately to a career change, but many do not. Some work callings immediately produce financial gains, but most won't. Listening to a work calling and choosing to follow it, wherever it might lead, teaches us to surrender our lives to the spiritual world. Putting our beliefs in action is a skill that helps us overcome our fears of uncertainty and discover our best selves in every area of our lives.

Work callings are spiritual experiences that build our trust to do what our soul feels called to do, as this will be the best thing for our lives.

WORK CALLINGS

Work callings are there to dare us to tap into our unique gifts. Each single work calling helps us pick up and refine new skills. Each one teaches us more about the desires of our soul. Each time we hear and follow a work calling, it prepares and leads us to our future callings and builds upon itself.

Might several work callings lead your character to a career change?

Yes, that's possible and even probable if the work we do right now brings us little enjoyment. It is likely we will start and keep heading in a different direction with each calling.

Might several work callings lead to a positive change in our financial status?

Yes, we might be called to things that bring financial success because of the gifts we have in that area.

We may also become inspired to reduce our consumption when we are more content with our daily life and this will increase our available financial resources.

Several work callings will undoubtedly leave a notable mark on our character's life in the human world, but we cannot predict how or when it will occur. Instead, we have to follow them one calling at a time and let it unfold. What we can control is whether our character's tactics are leading us to work where we will learn, practice, and be tested.

The whisper phase will lead your character to new places and eventually focus on a passion or two worth investing more time in. These may not be the passions you originally started exploring. Perhaps you followed your passion for golf, only to observe that it was the time outside that you craved more than the sport itself. Or perhaps you followed your desire for photography only to learn that it was the appreciation for the human form that you enjoyed more than the technical aspects of taking photos.

If we are patient, the whispers get louder and we'll start hearing more direction on where to go next. Hearing that direction is a sign that we are learning to listen. The next step is to learn how to follow. The reason we ignore our whispers of passions is often because we jump straight to the idea that we need to know exactly what the outcome will be to show up for the next step. We need to know where it is leading and want to be sure we will be successful in our endeavors.

The classroom of work challenges your character to show up in new places, without knowing why they are there and to things you may feel unprepared to succeed in. A calling is rooted in the desires of our soul, but that does not mean that we already have the skills to do the work we are called to. There is a good chance that we have spent our time building skills in things we were never called to. We have not been focusing our work lives on the things we most enjoy so we have not built knowledge and skills in those areas yet. That will come only from experience and practice.

This is why we need to follow the callings of our soul and not the assessments of our current skills. If we are called, we have to trust that we can and will build the skills needed along the way.

The classroom of work teaches us to practice anchoring our actions with what we believe. Every time we follow a calling, despite the vulnerability and uncertainty it brings, we grow stronger in our spiritual practice. Your character is willing to let your actions create the space to hear your callings. Your character is willing to show up and see where that leads you next.

YOUR CHOICE: TO SHOW UP

"Showing up" is a description of a physical act that moves our body from one place to another. We can hear the early whispers of a calling without going anywhere, but they won't get louder until we follow them to new places. Showing up tests our beliefs and proves whether we are learning to live them or not.

Our work classrooms are metaphors, but our work will take place through our physical mind and body. The first step is to listen. We have to take the actions that enable us to hear the whispers of a calling. The next step is to follow. Following a work calling means we have to get up and go somewhere. It is not enough to hear the calling. We have to pay attention to where we are being called to and show up there.

This book is my current work calling. I didn't show up when I first heard the calling to start writing. Truth be told, I heard the calling for a long time (years) before I did anything about it. Yet eventually, I started following the calling through the process of research and outlining, and eventually I showed up for the writing.

I am currently writing this book mainly from my home office in my basement between 5–7 a.m. every morning. Sometimes, I have to write from hotels when I am traveling for work. I write that early because I have work and family responsibilities that occupy much of my waking time. If you are like me, it was hard enough learning to hear my work calling in the first place, but showing up consistently is a real test. That was when I started to want to "leave my options open" and revert to a life that was easier. That was when I started to tell myself that I didn't need to write books and that my work life was good enough. I thought I could settle and not have to change my life so significantly. Yet, I was never fully content until I showed up for this calling.

Showing up is a skill that we are in the classroom of work to practice. Aligning our actions to our priorities almost always requires change.

We are learning not just how to say "Yes, I will follow you God" in our work, but how to say "Yes, I will follow you God" in all areas of our lives. We don't know where we are being led to, but if we truly trust the process we will not be afraid to go there anyway.

I don't know where any of my work is leading and neither will you. We can still happily follow God into the unknown world of work when we know that the spiritual growth we get from it is worth it.

Integrating our work into our spiritual practice makes them interdependent. Our work callings are only revealed to the extent that we remain in dialogue with God. If I need direction from God for a chapter I'm writing on a Tuesday, I cannot wait for a service on Sunday to seek spiritual counsel. Attempting to listen for and follow a work calling helps anchor our daily spiritual practice. It helps us learn what rituals bring us closer to God and what habits take us further away.

Each morning, I count on spiritual inspiration to direct the actions of my body and the workings of my mind.

In practical terms, that means I've had to stop sleeping with my phone on my nightstand. I noticed that when I did, I looked at it first thing in the morning instead of saying my prayers and meditating. My work calling requires that I get up and learn how to stay in dialogue with God, instead of getting up and choosing to be in dialogue with the world. My spiritual rituals have to come first if I hope to receive the inspiration and direction I desperately need to do my work.

That is the power of the classroom of work; it anchors our actions to what we believe. It teaches us how to get our work done. But I also find that, later in the day long after my work is complete, I still reap the benefits of having started my day anchored spiritually. I am a more patient parent. I am a more thoughtful and focused colleague. I am a loving partner. And I am a more compassionate and engaged citizen.

I don't have to tell you that learning to align your actions to your priorities comes up in many areas of life. For me, I used the skills I learned in the classroom of work to change other habits as well and show up where I wanted to be most.

Don't worry if you think that you have wasted time and missed opportunities to show up in the past. The beauty of life is that the only moment that matters is right now.

A work calling is a great place to learn to anchor your actions with what you believe. But remember that the first calling will be the hardest to hear. It is the time when you will be most inexperienced at being in dialogue with God. You will struggle to listen for and discern direction. You will hesitate to follow your work into uncertainty. You may not be willing to make all the changes needed to show up and test your faith. But next time, you will be much better prepared to hear your calling, follow it, and show up. Passing the test isn't the point. Being in the classroom is.

Seeking God, accepting uncertainty, and embracing change are lessons that will teach us not just how to work, but how to live. When we get that medical diagnosis that throws life upside down, we will have practiced the skill of taking the journey of sickness one step at a time. When we lose that loved one and can't imagine how we will go on, we will use the practice we got in the classroom of work to follow the uncertain path of grief. When our marriages are not playing out like we planned, we will know how to trust without fear of the potential outcomes. We will be okay. We will follow the path and trust that where it leads us is where we are meant to be.

The point is to use work as a means to teach us how to use our spiritual path to transform our life experience. Those benefits won't be limited to our work alone. Following a work calling is about showing up somewhere and learning to anchor our lives in our beliefs.

We don't enter the classroom of work to find success. We enter the classroom of work to live fulfilled in who we already are—our brilliant, buoyant and WHOLE soul.

CHAPTER 14

PURPOSE

The definition of purpose describes it as "the reason for which something is done or created or for which something exists." Working with purpose instills a deep motivation in us that anchors the resolve and persistence needed to follow our callings.

DISCOVERING OUR MOTIVATION

One of the things that surprised me about shifting my career from recruiting to coaching was how much more personal my relationship with each client is now. Certainly, recruiting required managing some of my candidates' personal situations—mainly reasons they could not relocate, had to relocate, or work/life balance concerns. But now, I spend a large portion of my time seeking to understand my clients' deeper motivations, which means first learning their personal stories to better understand their professional goals.

Many of the exercises we do together are meant to ask open-ended and unstructured questions to which I observe how they choose to interpret the question and what their responses provide and omit. The assumptions they make about what I'm looking for and the details they think are relevant to my understanding gives me a lot of insight into what motivates them and why.

For the same question, there are endless different answers. Even when clients have equivalent jobs in the same industry, they never tell their career stories similarly. One may tell an inspiring story about leadership and mentorship. One may tell an intellectually stimulating story about tackling the hardest problems. Yet another might tell a sadder story about doing what is expected of them or trying to cure the disease that could have saved someone they love.

I learn the most about my clients from understanding where their careers started and how they tell the story of their journey to date. I usually ask them

It is a myth that our work lives are relegated to our professional lives. Our work lives are inextricably tied with our personal experiences. A separate and isolated professional life does not exist.

to walk me through each work experience, one at a time, starting with how they picked their academic focus in school. That tends to be the first meaningful work choice represented on their resume. But I also instruct them to start earlier if relevant and to feel free to cover personal topics they wouldn't normally discuss in an interview.

THE QUESTION: WORK ON PURPOSE

In the course of telling me about their work lives, I have been trusted with stories of shame, fear, regret, tragedy, and trauma. In the last two years alone, I've heard excruciating stories about childhood illnesses, deaths of close family members (spouses, parents, siblings, and children), rape, extreme poverty, mental illness, physical illness, racism, and sexism.

When their stories aren't as disturbing, I see instead the kind of suffering that we try to ignore and leave unaddressed because we don't think it warrants the attention of a trauma. But there it is anyway, lingering and impacting my client's life and work choices. Stories that come up frequently are those that allude to an absent, self-centered, disapproving, or rigid parent; the regrets of our parents' lives that we take on as our burdens; a failing romantic life that breeds loneliness and shame, and undermines our power in our work life; a hidden but deep fear of inadequacy. All of these personal issues impact our professional lives.

I'm not sure I realized that these would be the kind of details I'd need to know to support my clients' careers, but it is now clear to me that there is no stronger calling to our work than to transform our personal pain into purpose. So often my job is to help my clients do just that and I know that my spiritual beliefs call me to do the same with my own pain as well.

If there is value in what you have endured, overcome, or been spared, are you willing to see and sit with the pain to transform it into purpose? There is a good chance it has already been calling you in some form. Have you been listening?

Are you willing to value your miraculous life enough to accept your imperfect history and transform it into a calling? If not, it will be a barrier to hearing, following, and doing the work that will fulfill you most. Throughout this chapter, frequently pause to ask yourself:

Q: Is my purpose anchored in what I believe?

And what do we believe? We believe that this life is a gift from God. Are we appreciating and honoring the value of that gift? The goal is to live fulfilled which is always a life lived with the authenticity of accepting our entire story and living with an open heart.

KEEPING AN OPEN HEART

Running from painful thoughts, or memories, requires that we keep a part of our hearts closed or hidden. Ignoring our pain leads us to disconnect with others, to love half-heartedly, to hide our truth and power. That is not a life anchored in what we believe.

Being called to a purpose is a thread that pulls us to use our pain to help others. It enables us to appreciate that there are sorrows in life that we can uniquely understand. This understanding equips us to do our work in a way that no one else could and makes the work meaningful. We don't uncover our purpose just because we know our painful stories. The question that leads to our work purpose isn't: what happened to me? It is: what skills or understanding do I have *because of* what happened to me?

As an example of how our pain can be transformed into a work purpose, imagine someone that is deeply drawn to a career that supports people who have a substance abuse issue. You may think someone like this has to have a personal experience with substance abuse. But that is not always the case. What they may have experienced instead was a time when they, or someone they loved desperately, needed a second (or even third) chance. They may have experienced a time when everyone seemed to have given up on them. A time when they had to live with the shame and consequence of their actions or when they felt deeply broken and flawed. They may know very well what it feels like to believe you have let everyone down and will never recover. And yet they did. So they know it is possible and they believe in the ability of others to do the same. This person has a unique gift to give those that are struggling with substance abuse. Their painful story has a purpose in their work. And boy, are we powerful in our work when we are able to channel that dirty, messy pain into something loving and pure.

EXERCISE

Take out your journal and consider the following questions:

- Has someone ever made you feel small?

- Have you ever felt invisible, inferior, unprepared, out of control, or hopeless?

- Have you done things you regret?

- Have you overcome something extraordinary?

- Have you escaped a path that others around you seemed destined for?

- Were you given a second chance you didn't deserve?

- Should your life have gone very differently, but miraculously it didn't?

Becoming aware of these experiences can be meaningful to your work. They can lead you to directly or indirectly help others.

Don't shy away from the above questions. If you have experienced a trauma you will probably find it easy to pinpoint your pain. But for others, you may have had the luxury of ignoring your pain. You may have been telling yourself for some time that everything is okay. But part of being alive is to have struggled with something. So don't shy away from the reflection on pain.

- What has life thrown at you in the past?
- What decisions would you do differently?
- What are you dealing with even right now?

Part of finding fulfillment in our work is to tap into our joy. The next and final chapter is all about that for good reason. Joyful living is the inevitable outcome of fully engaging in life. But there is no way to fully engage with life and ignore the part of life that includes pain and suffering. This chapter is about figuring out what to do with that pain. It is about exploring it, accepting it, and transforming it into something that heals more than just ourselves.

The story of our lives is our own personal hero's journey. The entire story can be told as a life lived with meaning if we choose to anchor our purpose with what we believe.

YOUR MEANING

Writers work to create characters that the show's viewers will relate to. If the viewer can put themselves in the same shoes as the character, they are more likely to connect emotionally with the show.

In the last two chapters, you defined what your character wants and how they plan to get it. Your character wants to stay on their spiritual journey and it is their most important goal. They want to use their work to achieve this. That is the "what" and "how" of what we want, but this chapter is meant to make clear "why" we want it in the first place. Exploring the "why" will not only help you better understand your character, but also help you find meaning in your character's role in the show.

We have an innate desire to work for a greater purpose and live for something outside of ourselves. Despite being drawn to a life of comfort and ease, we also have a strong attraction to the activities that transcend self-centered pursuits for a higher good. The draw to purpose is evident in many areas of human life. We can see it in our fascination with romantic relationships, to team sports, and even religion and spirituality itself. For all the claims that humans are selfishly motivated, we find it hard to live without purpose and meaning.

If you have ever fallen in love, you know that during the early infatuation stage, you feel almost invincible. In this state, we appear to have special powers to rise above our normal fears and selfish needs. Even basic necessities like sleep and food can be reduced while we focus on this new relationship. It feels as if we might be capable of loving another person so much that we can transcend our faults, our pain, and our barriers to intimacy. We take our loneliness and fear of inadequacy, and we begin to transform it with the purpose of loving another.

EXPERIENCING TRANSCENDENCE

Romantic love serves as an example of our desire to transcend our human selves by seeking a higher purpose. We are drawn to the power of something that we care about so deeply that it might help us break the bondage of our pain and transform into the glorious loving and powerful being we suspect lurks inside.

We hope that our new relationship might help us rise above our struggles with humility, surrender, gratitude, discipline, connection, love, power, and/or patience. Where we struggle in any one of these beliefs, we hope to find the strength to overcome that weakness in an effort to build a lasting union. Deep down we hope our new love will help us to get (or keep us) on track spiritually, living a life powered from our soul. It is no wonder that we seek to find a soulmate.

It is possible to enter the classroom of marriage and grow spiritually there, but it is not as easy as riding the chemical highs that new love might imply. That however, doesn't stop us from repeatedly trying to harness the power of purpose to transform us in each subsequent new relationship.

We get a glimpse of this transcendence even when we watch our team win a championship. They have brought every skill to the table and put aside their individual needs to be a part of something meaningful. At times, it appears as if they gain miraculous abilities because of it. We are in awe of championships because they represent more than winning. They represent transcendence.

The desire to live for a higher purpose is so strong that we are never at peace until we find it. It may lead us to pursue multiple romantic relationships or endless achievements, leaving our bodies and minds exhausted. We may think that it is belonging or success that we desire most, but rarely is that enough to be at peace. Some part of us will always be restless until we find meaning in the things we pursue.

This is where your character has the opportunity to seek a life of meaning and do work that has a purpose. The transcendence we seek can indeed be found in the classroom of work if we commit to finding it there.

If we study any spiritual tradition, it will inevitably lay out a path to live in the beliefs outlined in Part I. Understanding universal beliefs is not hidden knowledge nor difficult to understand. Finding the path to fulfillment is not the hard part, following it and transforming our lives is.

The reason we seek out a calling is because we desire to do work for something that is larger than ourselves and meaningful enough to help us stay motivated on our spiritual path. We want to unite our life's work with our soul's work.

The calls on your character's life will require that you give more than you ever imagined you could. Work done in our callings is where we find our unique greatness. It is not the kind of greatness that is rooted in the idea of perceiving ourselves as better or more special than others. We may never score the winning points in a championship and hear the crowds chanting our names.

It is the kind of greatness that illuminates the miraculous capabilities of our unique soul. It is the kind of greatness that we get a glimpse of briefly in early romantic relationships. For a little while, we are at our very best: kind, loving, energetic, and serving others. We show another who we can be when we are willing to take down our walls and reveal our unique, tender, and authentic self.

Finding meaning in our pain and dedicating the work of our lives to a higher purpose allows for more than those brief glimpses of greatness in ourselves; it allows us the opportunity to live connected to it and harness its power.

Our character can transcend our limitations in the pursuit of work when it is tied to something we are emotionally connected to. We don't want to merely do work to make a living. Your character wants to let the work call you to something greater. Work tied to a purpose can call us to reveal the best of our souls. It can call us to reveal and set free parts of us that are hidden, tied down, or seemingly lost forever.

Work transforms us when it gives us the motivation to grow spiritually. Work transforms us when it unites us with our souls and reveals what we truly want from our lives. Work transforms us when it teaches us to value our appearance in this show of life enough to fully engage with all parts of our experience.

Spiritual transformation is what we want but transcending our human self for a life of purpose is why we want it.

YOUR CHOICE:
TO EMBRACE YOUR STORY

I'd like to share with you the story that called me to my purpose. It is not an especially rare story. I realize that many people share a similar story, but the impact it has had on my unique work path has been deeply meaningful to me.

It started when I was 17 years old. What I saw as my never-ending sadness was actually a mental health crisis. One night after a breakup with a boyfriend, I made the decision to end my life. These were thoughts I had harbored for some time without anyone knowing. Whenever I hit an especially rough patch I would fantasize about not having to live with myself anymore. Not having to hear my thoughts. Not having to make others put up with me. I fantasized that on the other side of my death the pain of being me would end.

I went into the basement where my grandfather was living with us and took a bottle of his blood pressure medication. I don't remember if I knew it was blood pressure medication at the time or if I just assumed that any prescription drug taken in a large enough quantity would end my life.

In any event, I laid out the contents of the entire bottle, or at least what was left of it, on our coffee table. I remember staring at the pills for a long time. I looked at the pile and thought about how my life sat in the mound. There it was, the difference between life and death.

I questioned myself about whether I was truly ready. Did I even have the courage to follow through with it? I gave no thoughts to family or friends that might be impacted by my death. It just wasn't on my mind, even though both my parents were asleep in the house at the time and would have found me in the morning. I could only think of ending my pain. The illness in my mind continued to challenge me to "have the nerve" for once to follow through with something.

I sat on the couch and wrestled with those thoughts for some time. It has been decades now, so I don't fully remember just how long I stared at the pills. All I know is that I kept weighing the pain of my existence against the fear of dying. I thought about how hard it was to live with my inadequacies. How hard it was to deal with how I could never seem to be who I wanted to be.

My mind kept reminding me that I had been living with this struggle since childhood and that it would never go away. I was the bossy child, the high-maintenance child, and the child that caused my mother to have gray hair. But I had tried to fix myself and just couldn't seem to do it. I wondered, "Why couldn't I get better at being who I wanted to be? Why was I born so flawed? Is there any point in me being alive?" I remember having a lot of questions that felt unanswerable.

Though I couldn't have known it then, these moments in my history would become highly relevant to my purpose and the callings to my work later in life. Yet at the time, even the mental debate felt hopeless. Not being able to take the pills felt like another unbearable failure. I just wanted the struggle to be over.

I did go ahead and take the pills that night. All of them. But clearly, I am still here to tell this story. However, I have never understood how I survived that night, when so many others are successful. They aren't rushed to the hospital in time. They aren't saved. They will never have the second chance that I am now living.

Over the years, I have been impacted by the suicide of others. I have watched as their loved ones struggled in agony to make sense of why such a beautiful life with so much potential ended. Observing their pain is astounding. It is relentless and never ending. I have felt an enormous amount of guilt that I walk this earth still and many others do not. That their families were given a life sentence of grief and mine wasn't. I questioned what value could come from my experience and resisted exploring it. I preferred to think I had "moved on."

Revisiting our painful histories is a hard thing to do. Even writing this story all these years later was difficult. These memories can be excruciating, and so full of guilt and shame, that we frequently fail to explore them.

"Why am I here?" is the question that slowly gets revealed when we choose to anchor our purpose in what we believe and let it guide us to our work.

You may never experience mental illness— certainly, I hope you don't. You may not have ever attempted suicide, but I am certain you have a history of your own. You have had struggle, heartache, trauma, or pain of some sort in your life. That is a certainty. But what value could come from it? How could that history be used to help others?

I want to be clear that I don't believe God chooses to give us trauma or pain to prepare us for our work. There is no silver lining to suffering, violence, or hardship, and these things are not a blessing in themselves. Yet part of living in an unjust, man-made world often includes exposure to things we must overcome or endure. We can transform our suffering into purpose by exploring what hurt us in the past, or still hurts us today, and looking for ways to use the experience for the benefit of others.

For me, my life's purpose is to help others find meaning in their lives (often through guiding their work choices). Perhaps more than most people, I have had an intimate view into how painful living with hopelessness and emptiness can be. I haven't been called to work dealing directly with mental illness or suicide prevention. But I now see that I am called to work that seeks to help people appreciate the value of their lives.

Despite my history of hopelessness, or perhaps because of it, this work fulfills me like nothing else ever has. If this book helps you find greater meaning in your life, that was indeed my purpose.

EXERCISE

Take out your journal and write down whatever comes to mind about your history.

- What have you made it through?
- What have you endured?
- What experiences have others been blessed with that you were denied?
- What is painful about how your life has turned out like it has?

These do not have to be traumatic memories, but they may be. Or you may explore why you were granted such grace when others were not. Either way, you have had a front-row seat at observing and understanding something that not everyone knows nor appreciates.

· What can you do with that knowledge?

Anchoring your purpose in what you believe is not about trying to answer these questions quickly. It is about making sure that you keep asking them and are committed to following wherever they might lead you.

CHAPTER 15

JOY

Joy is best described by the intense feeling of connection with life itself. To be joyful is to bring fresh fascination and awe to each moment. Joy differs from happiness in that it is not dependent on our circumstances, but instead anchors us in the glorious nature of simply being alive.

CONNECTING TO JOY

I think it is fair to say that most (if not all) of my clients are accomplished in their careers. They have pursued many of the career objectives that society considers markers of success (i.e. fancy degrees, impressive titles, and comfortable compensations). Conventional wisdom assumes that once we achieve these standards, we will be happy in our work lives. Yet, that is not the case.

One client in particular sticks out in my mind. His resume was flawless. He graduated from one of the best business schools. He reached the executive level at an early age. He was, at the time, being offered a significant leadership position in the industry of his choice. My job was to help him decide if he should take this offer. It was clearly a rare job opportunity.

My concern *wasn't* with the job itself. Truth be told, it was an amazing career opportunity and the kind of offer that doesn't come up very often. Yet, he clearly *wasn't* excited about it. You could hear the tension in his voice when he discussed it. And, as I began to dig deeper into his work history, it became obvious that this was a pattern. He hadn't been excited about his work life for some time.

His approach to work was to endure difficult and mostly uninspiring assignments for the outcome of greater financial reward and achievement. He chose these kinds of opportunities over and over again. At one point, I asked him to describe for me the work projects he'd enjoyed the most and the ones he'd disliked. It was easy for him to tell me which ones he'd disliked, but he struggled to answer when asked what he'd enjoyed. Instead, he gave me examples of times when he'd had "the most impact." He explained that after long periods of grueling work, he was proud of the results of those projects.

So my question for him was whether he planned to continue this pattern of simply enduring for the benefit of maintaining his trajectory of success. Was he satisfied that he had achieved enough to choose work that brought him joy or would he continue to endure until he retired?

You might be reading this and thinking that choosing to live a better life experience is an easy decision, but it wasn't. On the one hand, he had a real offer he would have to decline. To decline that offer seemed illogical and it had been so long since he did work that inspired him that he frankly questioned whether finding joy in his work was even possible. In the end, he took the offer.

THE QUESTION: THRIVING WITH JOY

Our final question tests what we believe. Our spiritual beliefs call us to honor the gift of life. They call us to cherish that gift enough to enjoy it. When we truly anchor our lives in what we believe we are not willing to settle for simply enduring. We challenge ourselves to thrive in all areas of our life. We refuse to settle for less than joyful living. So, ask yourself the following question as you move through this chapter, but more importantly as you move through the days of your life:

Q: Is my joy anchored in what I believe?

Do you even know what your joy is? Do you know what your joy feels like? How joy comes to you? What drains your joy?

For my client, he was so disconnected from joy that he couldn't imagine prioritizing it over the work struggles that were so familiar. He doubted his decision to take the offer, but he took it anyway. He was prepared to push himself to endure each and every day. He knew that he was "successful" in his career, but he also knew that he wasn't happy or satisfied with his life.

When our soul can't trust us to listen for our deepest desire for joy, doubt and inertia will be present in our decisions. We may wonder why we can't reach contentment with work that should be "good enough" or why we can't seem to get motivated about the things we say we want to achieve. These are signs that our work lives are not anchored in joy.

When we are working whole, it feels like a joy and honor to be doing our work. Both the soul and the human self are getting what they want, and we are living a life of fulfillment and meaning.

FINDING JOY IN YOUR CALLINGS

Our work should be a manifestation of who we are and what we believe. Often when life is stagnating, unfulfilling, or inauthentic we see it in multiple areas of our lives. It shows itself in our finances, our relationships, our spiritual lives, and our work. Sometimes our pain leads us to look for a new job because it is a quick fix. We seek a job change when what we really want is to integrate and anchor what we believe into the rest of our life. We want to live a soulful existence that is true to who we are and meaningful.

Our lives are indeed short, but we get many chances to get up and face a new day. It is probable that you will get up tomorrow, and the next day, and the day after that. Time is limited, but most of us get an unfathomable number of hours to do work in our lives. What makes a life fulfilled is when we align our work pursuits with the things that bring us joy.

We shouldn't have to force ourselves to focus on a true work calling. We might have to push ourselves to stay on task some days, but the focus it holds in our lives should stem from the joy it brings us. Hearing the early whispers of that calling starts with noticing the desires of your soul and when you feel most alive and why. If you stay in dialogue with God, your calling will grow more and more joyful with every step you make toward it. This is not a subtle feeling. When you do the work you are supposed to be doing, you feel an exhilarated connection to who you truly are.

What if doing your work fed you with energy instead of draining it? What if your work was highly inspiring instead of an obligation? How might that change your ability to enjoy your life experience?

We pursue a work calling so we can shift our days toward inspired and joyful living. Most, if not all, of that shift has to do with uncovering our gifts and using them to serve a greater cause. I am intentionally using the word "uncovering" because it takes time to explore and find your gifts. We have to make the connection between what brings us joy and where we have talents (once properly developed) that the world needs.

You know you have found a work calling when you no longer view your days off with anticipation. You should definitely be making time to rest, but you are doing that as part of the overall plan to increase and preserve your capacity. You are not using rest as an escape or break from labor. You are using it as a part of the natural rhythm to grow.

Think about the freedom that comes from this type of work. Many people think they will wait until the end of their lives to do the work they enjoy. They think they will wait until all their other financial needs have been met to focus on fulfillment. But that isn't the sacred life experience our beliefs should be leading us to.

WORKING WHOLE

I can always tell when someone shifts to working whole. They don't need to tell me that they feel a deeper connection to the work because I sense it in their energy. They seem different from who they were before. They are more present and authentic. They are braver and more vulnerable. They have a focus and clarity in their plans and are at ease with the uncertainty ahead. They are in full engagement with the experience of their lives. They are fulfilled by the pursuit of this joyful work.

Spiritually, I can feel the power of their extraordinary energy. Yet, in the human world I can see the results of their increased capacity to work. Tactically, they are actually logging more hours of work than others and therefore getting much more done. But they barely notice it because the work is feeding them energy.

They have reduced the separation between "worktime" and "playtime." They find their work inspirations during their prayer or leisure time, which in some ways makes it worktime as well. They feel inspired to do extra tasks in the early morning, late at night, or on the weekends simply because they want to. They feel better after working because work is a source of energy not a drain. And they better prioritize rest because they know that fresh thinking is needed to chart the course.

On the contrary, I know many people that are highly successful and exhausted. They have achieved success by conventional standards and are posed to continue that trajectory. Yet, their energy takes great effort to sustain. They have frequent highs and lows and never seem to be satisfied with the success they have. That is what living without joy does to our energy. Many of us get stuck here—measuring our results, but never being fulfilled.

Without joy, we feel stuck in our current careers. Many of our initial work callings start as side projects, volunteer efforts, or hobbies. This work has to be done outside of our paying jobs and requires that we find the time and energy to do additional work. Following those kinds of work callings are only possible when we are doing work that brings us joy.

Choosing the joyful living that comes from working whole seems like a no-brainer, but living this way is a daring choice. Like anything worth having, there will be obstacles in the way, so we have to be prepared to over-come them.

YOUR OBSTACLES

There is only one question left to answer about your char-acter. What must you overcome to get what you want?

There is always something stopping us from achieving our goals. In acting that is called the character's "obstacle." Our goals can be thwarted by another character, a circumstance in the storyline, or an internal conflict. The purpose of identifying the obstacles are so we can be better prepared to overcome them.

This final chapter points us back to the beginning of the book. There are many things that stand in the way of living our beliefs. Each of us will struggle with different things at various times. But living the script of our beliefs allows us the awareness to identify obstacles and embrace the opportunity for growth that they inevitably bring.

The goal of your character is to live a full and meaningful life. To do that, you'll have to commit to the daily process of weaving your beliefs into your life decisions. We are attempting to live in a new show. But first, we have to stop living in the old show. Your old show may have been a drama or a thriller. It may have had you cast as the main character and been set in your comfortable bubble. Choosing to create and live in your new show will lead to a more fulfilled existence but getting there will create significant challenges and the need to realign many parts of your life.

Each single work calling will push us to walk further on our spiritual path. Along the way what we should be doing will be revealed to us, but also who we are and why we are living in this season of the show. Those revelations will invite us to live as the person we truly are, rather than accommodating who we thought we were supposed to be.

To be clear, the pursuit of fulfillment is a privilege. If you are struggling with a need for satisfaction and meaning in your work that means you are not struggling with your most basic needs for survival. It probably also means that you have a reasonable amount of security and belonging already. Those privileges alone are enough to inspire your character to give their highest service back to the world.

One of the biggest obstacles your character will face is the challenge of inviting contentment into life. Contentment is not an attribute our society seems to honor but something your character must embrace to stay on script. Contentment goes against everything the human world has taught us about success. Yet, contentment is an essential part of joyful living. We have been led to believe that more is always better, but that idea robs us of the possibility of fulfillment. To be "full" is to be satisfied with what you have already.

DEFINING SUCCESS

Prior to anchoring my life with my beliefs, I made most of my work decisions in the hope of becoming more "successful" and financially comfortable. Living our spiritual beliefs means that we don't need to seek our identity and worth from outside sources. We can live complete and whole with a life anchored spiritually. But that doesn't mean ignoring our worldly responsibilities. Bills still have to get paid to provide us shelter and providing the body with food is essential. Working toward a calling is not about ignoring our financial needs. It is doing the work it takes to cultivate an orientation toward contentment, which then paves the way to following our joy.

Would your character choose to run a race without knowing the distance or where the finish line is? It would make running the race extremely difficult because they wouldn't know how much energy to put out at any given time. They wouldn't know if they were close to the end and should be sprinting or if they had miles to go and should be conserving energy.

Working for a higher purpose demands that we decide where the finish line for our human needs is, so we can succeed in anchoring our lives in joy. Your character has to live with fulfilled joyful living as the only definition of success, so they must assess their lifestyle needs to use their time, money, and energy efficiently toward meeting that goal.

Our lifestyle needs are personal decisions and often fluctuate in different life stages. But you don't want to spend more time and money maintaining a lifestyle than you actually need to live in joy and contentment. Your approach to consumption will impact your ability to pursue new and bolder work callings. That doesn't mean we will all be satisfied with the same finish line—it just means that we all need to set one for ourselves.

What complicates our consumption needs is that many of us use material possessions and financial status symbols as a replacement for finding peace, meaning, or enjoyment elsewhere. Retail therapy is a real thing. We get an emotional jolt from purchasing a new item and that feeling can help us temporarily cope when living inauthentic or uninspired days.

But how does this impact the episodes of our lives? When your character is content, they can stop purchasing new things and save more money to invest in a business venture. They may be able to save for an unpaid sabbatical at their job or another degree. They may be able to take on a lower-paying apprenticeship to break into the field of work that brings them joy. These are the kind of decisions that intersect with the spiritual world and the human world.

Our soul will call us to joy, but whether we are willing to follow it sometimes depends on our human lifestyle.

In a culture where we are always expected to want more, it is life changing to arrive at a place of contentment. The sooner we can get there, the freer we are to creatively redirect our resources and time. Your character will choose their best daily life experience over any generic expectations of what success has to be. The part of us that wants to live our episodes honoring the gift of life deeply desires to choose joyful days over enduring work for the sake of success.

Assess whether some of your lifestyle choices may be there to help you cope with what is not meaningful nor fulfilling in your life. Consider if you would need all that you have if you enjoyed your daily experience more.

Our human lives require money and material things. We cannot completely ignore that while walking a spiritual path. Yet the calling journey requires that we get comfortable with the idea that we can't control everything, including our financial prosperity. We can't guarantee that the business we are called to start will be an immediate financial success. We can't guarantee that the new career path will accelerate our earning potential.

Satisfaction is a simple comparison of how much we have versus how much we think we need. Most of us have spent our lives striving to have more without ever trying to need less. Yet, that is the part of the equation that your character can control the most.

Failing to assess your lifestyle needs is an important obstacle to overcome. That is not to say that you will have to settle long term for your minimum bar. It only means that you will be free to make decisions based on what honors your life and leads you to joy.

You may still live and earn well above your minimum bar in the long run. Those working whole have a way of inadvertently generating abundance because they are effortlessly working more and at their highest potential. But that's an outcome we can't predict, nor do we want to live with our self-worth tied to it. Loving our days, meeting our needs, and putting meaningful work into the world will fulfill us regardless. Cultivating contentment empowers your character to play their role in your show perfectly.

YOUR CHOICE: TO SEE THE MIRACLE OF LIFE

I had a family friend die suddenly a few years ago. I remember so much about the day he died. What I was wearing, what the weather was like on that beautiful August day. Who told me and how hard my mind resisted the reality of that unbelievable news.

Until then, all the deaths in my life had been people that were reasonably old or somewhat anticipated.

His death was shockingly sudden, unthinkable, and created spiritual questions I had never asked before. Most notably, I started to wonder exactly where he had gone. I understood where my religion said he was, and I understood where his religion said he was. Those were different places and even those places were hard for me to imagine. I seemed to want to know if I could still access any connection to him. Was the end of his life really the end of our relationship?

I couldn't imagine that I would never again be in his presence. Never. His spirit was such a gift that I had an unbearably hard time believing it was gone forever. I have other relationships that are much closer than the one I had with him, but he had the kind of impact on people that was unforgettable.

I still don't know where he is, and I imagine that I never will in this life. But the act of questioning made me start frequently looking up at the sky purely out of instinct. I started looking up during my morning commute, especially when I would get to the exits closest to where he had lived, and I would wonder aloud... "Where are you?"

Then something interesting started to happen. I realized that I had never paid much real attention to the sky. Maybe occasionally on an extraordinary day when I was off work and fully relaxed. But now I was staring at the sky every day, multiple times a day. I was looking for something though I am still not sure what exactly.

The sky is an astounding miracle. I could not believe I had never appreciated it before. It is intensely beautiful, frequently different, and mesmerizing. Even those descriptors fail to do it any justice. When I look at the sky now, I feel that I am with his presence somehow. I see something beautiful that is far away. I can experience it from where I am, but it is not mine to keep close. That is part of the awe of life that joyful living creates room for.

Simple and pure experiences cost us nothing and we cannot own them. Yet, they are always available to inspire and heal us. Spiritual lessons come to us from many classrooms and I am grateful that the classroom of grief taught me an important lesson about appreciating the beauty of life.

INSIDE THE CLASSROOM OF WORK

The classroom of work seeks to teach us similar lessons. In our attempt to follow our callings, we deepen our connection with awe and beauty. We look into the human world with new eyes which are capable of seeing the spiritual world sitting right alongside it. We look at human beings with a renewed ability to see the God-given blessings of a human life with all the unique and spectacular possibilities. We look upon the present moment as the only moment that matters to our work.

Joy gives us the opportunity to appreciate and honor our sacred time to be alive. Appreciating the miraculous moments of life strengthens our connection to the life force that is within us. Feeling the awesome power that lives in us with each breath is what helps us enjoy our days. Before the big miracles start falling into place, we have to see the small ones. We have to see the joy in the normal yet miraculous moments of our life. There are many simple pleasures we miss out on when we fail to be in touch with joyful living.

We fail to notice the beauty of the trees outside the window or the exhilarating feel of the breeze. We miss the little drops of condensation that form on a glass or the exquisite shine of a copper mug. You likely know what it tastes like, but do you know what pepper smells like? Do you like the sound of ice cubes shaking in a glass? What does it feel like to sneeze? Words can never fully describe these experiences. They have to be lived and that is the magic of them. All these small, awesome, and frequently unnoticed parts of our days remind us of the joy it is to simply be alive.

Joy leads us to spiritual growth because it reminds us to see the beauty in ourselves and in this life experience. It reminds us not to waste our chances to enjoy life because it is too precious to do so.

EXERCISE

As a final exercise, take a sheet of paper and draw a line or fold it down the middle.

On the right side of the paper write "What brings me joy?"

On the left side write "What takes joy from me?"

Then write down whatever comes to mind.

This list is your starting place to listening for your joy. Keep this list and work to spend more of your days on the right side of the column than the left. With every step toward something on the list, pay attention to what you are feeling (not thinking). Is the pull growing stronger or remaining the same? Some joys will not be work related, but they are still important in your spiritual journey. They are helping you live fulfilled.

There will be clues about your callings as you pursue a more joyful life experience. You are listening for greater clarity on what kind of work gives your spirit joy simply by doing it or being around it and what drags your spirit down. It is a data-gathering exercise on what your soul wants to be around and not a career-planning tool.

Resist the urge to focus too quickly on things that are jobs or outcomes you seek versus things that can only be experienced in the present moment. An example would be noticing you enjoy the beauty of natural wood instead of jumping to plans to sell furniture. The point is to discover what kind of experiences feel good to you in the present moment without any thought about outcomes.

Remember also that you are exploring your joy, not your biggest strength. Only focus on what inspires you. As you build your list consider the following questions:

- What are the things you cannot stop yourself from doing or topics you keep exploring because you enjoy them so much?
- What do you do in your spare time or add on to your work responsibilities when they are not in the job description?
- What are the things that make you most upset when they are not done properly?
- What kind of problems in the world cross your mind most frequently or bother you the most?

This exercise will help to start to alert you to the clues embedded in your soul about what you will enjoy working on. You may have some ideas that come to mind right away. However, many of us have suppressed some of our passions because long ago we decided they wouldn't make us enough money or were unrealistic. Getting in dialogue with God will open your heart and mind enough to reveal these suppressed passions to you.

Embracing joy will require that you identify with multiple interests and work to spend more time around them. Not more time thinking, researching, or talking about them, but more time *doing* them. Make the time to explore your interests, find people that enjoy them equally, and see if that level of passion subsides, sustains, or grows.

You are looking to see not only if you enjoy it, but how much you enjoy it. You are listening to hear when one passion motivates you to devote time to it above the others. That is not the same as deciding that one passion is easier to pursue as a career or that one passion has a clear path to starting a business venture. The only thing you are seeking to hear is: What brings me the most joy? What is God trying to tell me about who I am and who am I here to help?

If you have been struggling to hear your callings for some time, you may wonder why this discovery process will be any different from previous attempts. Perhaps you have created lists and given lots of thought to what you enjoy, only to feel confused or unmotivated. Perhaps you thought you had identified your passion, but then found yourself unmotivated to follow it. The key is remembering that you did those processes before you fully anchored your life in what you believe. You did this process without embracing contentment and prioritizing joyful days and spiritual growth above all else.

You are now living anchored in a life that is opening you up mentally and emotionally to a different experience. You are living in greater connection with humanity which means you are letting problems and emotions in that you were previously blocking. You are better at knowing what you feel than you used to be.

You are focused on growth. You are living in greater discipline, allowing yourself the freedom to change, and releasing the attachments that made you afraid to be bold. You are resisting the urge to plan and instead patiently following your beliefs in the knowledge that they will lead you to where you need to be.

It is a brand new "you" that you are bringing to this process. You are bringing someone who will be more creative, informed, observant, and open-hearted. You will also find yourself in different places having very different experiences. That will bring new data. This is a discovery process unlike any you have attempted in the past. You have the opportunity to tap into extraordinary energy and live your days anchored to joy.

Are you ready to get to work? Are you ready to cherish your life? Are you ready to be working whole?

CONCLUSION

YOUR COMMUNITY

When our lives are fully integrated and anchored in what we believe, we can create work from a place of wholeness. Bringing our full spiritual self into our human reality leads to a life of meaning and purpose. Your work can provide some of the most joyful experiences of your life and I hope this book is the spark that starts your journey. Along the way, you will need a community of support so that is the final topic to cover in conclusion.

Few among us are born into a large community that is both accepting of who we are and able to grow with us spiritually. Most of us have to do some extra work to build our fullest sense of community.

Living our beliefs and working whole will reveal who we truly are to the world. It will naturally attract the people that should be in our community. Yet, one of the hardest parts of building community is finding the space to let new people into our lives and letting others leave or play a diminished role. So, in conclusion, I want to encourage you to be thoughtful about the community you are building and the support you will need for the work ahead.

Imagine yourself living in two different moments. In moment A, there has been a bad storm and the electricity is out. You turn on a flashlight to navigate your way to the kitchen. The light of the flashlight is strong and prominent as it cuts through the darkness.

In moment B, there has also been a storm and again the electricity is out, but this time it is during the daytime. The windows are uncovered and there is bright light shining throughout the entire house. You turn on the flashlight, but it seamlessly blends with the bright light of the room. You can barely tell that the flashlight is even on and you definitely don't need it to find the kitchen.

Clearly, the flashlight is playing a more important role in moment A. But what if our goal was to find the kitchen? Which moment would it be easier to do in?

These two moments mirror our experiences with the people in our lives. We may feel more important when we have to light our own path through the darkness, but we will walk the spiritual path faster and better when we surround ourselves with a community that brings their own light into our lives.

BUILDING YOUR COMMUNITY

Living in your truth is not always easy when it comes to building a community. If you have spent a good deal of your life showing the world a version of yourself that is incomplete or false, then it is likely that you have attracted several relationships that are not authentic to who you are. Through the process of attracting and building your community, you'll have to continue to live in power with the strength to handle any rejection or loss that comes from inauthentic connections falling away or being minimized.

Having a strong community will feed your spiritual growth and enhance your work. It will also reinforce your strength to live in power and keep you on script.

We want to find our people because they will enhance everything about our life experiences and our work.

There are three types of people that will make up your community. Hopefully, many of the people already in your life will serve in these roles. If not, you need to look out for new relationships you can build. Finding your people will not only help you see your path more clearly, but it will shape your journey.

Ideally, you want to attract and embrace people that fit into the following categories:

- Sustainers
- Mentors
- Workmates

SUSTAINERS

A sustainer is someone that helps you stay anchored in the spiritual world. They share similar beliefs and are working just as hard to live them out. They may not serve as guides to your work callings, but when you are struggling to live your beliefs, these people will help you persevere. They are running in the same race and on the same team, working to be better and to make the world a better place.

Being part of a religious community doesn't guarantee that you have these people around you. You have to build relationships with individuals to discern if they are truly able to *live* what they study. There are some obvious signs that should help you discern who is living anchored in their beliefs. Nobody lives with perfection, but here are a few things to pay attention to when looking for your sustainers:

- Kindness to all
- Joyful energy
- Compassionate and flexible thinking toward others
- Peaceful spirits
- Authentic interactions

These traits go beyond whether you can talk with them about the tenets of your spiritual practice or celebrate the same religious holidays. You are looking for evidence that they are choosing to live in humility, surrender, discipline, gratitude, connection, love, power, and patience.

You are looking for the people that don't delight in the pain or missteps of others. They are slow to speak a bad word about anyone. You are looking for those that can see value in the lives of imperfect people. Sustainers don't need prestige nor titles to jump in and help others. They aren't looking for opportunities to impose their convictions or will on anyone. They are not even sure if their opinion is definitely the correct one. They change their minds about things and people. They know they are not here to be the judge of others and they focus on the work of their lives instead.

You are looking for the people you feel good being around. They are relaxed and seem to enjoy life. Finally, you are looking for people that are comfortable being themselves. They are not guarded. They are not projecting an image they want you to see. They are able to show their flaws and accept the flaws of others. These people will help sustain you and you will need as many of these people as you can find. They are rare. You will also need to *be this person* for others. Your show needs more of these characters.

Revealing our true selves isn't easy. We worry about being judged and we worry about failing, not just the expectations of others but our own too. We need sustainers in our community to give us a safe place to let our true nature come out and risk vulnerability. The more we reveal who we are, the more sustainers we will attract. Having sustainers in your community is like having the proper soil for your seeds to grow. They feed us and help us blossom.

MENTORS

Mentors have embraced the lessons taught in the classroom of work and will intimately understand the work journey you are about to go on. They are important in helping you to navigate the two worlds—the spiritual and the human. It is great to get advice from successful people that know how to achieve things in the human world, but you are looking to take a path that is different. You do not want to merely be successful, you want to be fulfilled.

Someone who has walked that path before will better understand what is out of your control, what needs to be surrendered, and what you can influence if you can keep yourself from going off-script. A mentor is not going to try to send you down the exact path they have traveled, but instead they are going to help you steer your own path. You need a mentor when following a work calling because a mentor will have a much higher risk tolerance than most people around you.

These are the people you can come to with your most bold work ideas. These are the people who will not need you to have worked out every step before you can get started. They know how to navigate between the spiritual and the human world. They trust the power of passion as a call. Some of the things you start pursuing during your discovery phase are things that may seem fruitless or even crazy to others. If you have a good mentor that has walked this journey, they will be supportive when others struggle to trust your process.

WORKMATES

This category is the hardest to attract and maintain. I could write an entire book on the topic alone, but I'll cover it briefly here because it is too important to our work lives to leave out. Workmates (our significant others and primary relationships) have a substantial impact on our calling journey. Choosing them wisely and/or improving our relationships with them is a major way to influence where the work of our lives can lead.

You don't have to have a workmate to manifest your body of work. Some callings may even be easier to navigate without being encumbered by someone that has their work callings intertwined with yours. However, if you do have a primary relationship (spouse, partner, significant other, or any other relationship you must make joint life decisions with), it is important that that person be a workmate. A workmate goes beyond romantic feelings and focuses on the aspect of love that is rooted in honoring human potential.

The workmate relationship doesn't mean that the other person has to sacrifice their work callings to help you follow yours or vice versa. It means that you have someone else that is committed to the journey of growing spiritually and honoring the potential of both of your lives. This is especially important as workmates weigh in on many lifestyle decisions that impact the work we can get done. If you have a life partner, you are not free to make lifestyle decisions completely on your own and you will live with the decisions that you two come up with jointly.

Workmates have a significant impact on the kind of work we can get done over our lives. For that reason, choosing a workmate is one of the largest work decisions you will ever make.

If you have not already chosen your workmate, here are a few things you need to consider:

- ## Do you share similar spiritual beliefs?

  That will tell you if you will be living out a similar script and attempting to navigate both the spiritual and human world together. Someone who is only navigating the human world will struggle to under stand the value of being in the classroom of work. They will unintentionally create obstacles and breed doubt in your journey. Workmates don't need to practice the same religion, but it is very important to be living out the same core beliefs.

- ## Do you have similar levels of what it will take to satisfy your material needs?

  Finding a workmate with a somewhat similar view on how much is "enough" in the human world (no matter what that is) is important. That means that you have to first do the work to even know what your level of "enough" is. If you are still taking on society's view that "more" is always better, you first have to cultivate your own idea of what will be enough for you. Your potential partner has to do the same on their own to even begin accessing if your answers are compatible. Have those discussions and do that soul-searching *before* committing to a lifelong workmate. It will impact your work options greatly.

- **Would a scenario where your workmate doesn't live up to their full potential in life be as hard to bear as a scenario where you don't live up to yours?**

  If the answer is yes, then you will have the necessary commitment to create a joint plan. Be honest with yourself about this question. Sometimes the deep-down answer is no. You may value this person, but you don't love them enough to put their needs equal to your own. This is probably not a person you will be inspired enough to be a workmate to. Acknowledge that in truth and power and free them to find the workmate they deserve. Free yourself from having to live in guilt when you fail to love them well.

In some seasons, it may seem that only one workmate gets to be in the classroom of work, but that will always need to be a joint decision on what is best for you both and motivated from genuine love. Finding a person that can partner with you long term isn't easy. You want to be with someone that catches your eye and makes your heart jump but be sure to choose a workmate that can create a meaningful life experience with you too.

If you have already chosen a workmate and worry that they are not aligned with the list above the best place to start assessing and working on that is in Part I of this book.

Romantic love is its own spiritual classroom. Living out our beliefs in our primary relationship has a power to transform our lives. It won't fix everything if you two are truly not compatible or they are not willing to do any work with you. And certainly not if you are facing any level of abuse. But in some cases, just having one partner choose to live in the eight beliefs in Part I can transform their primary relationship into something new.

Before you decide that your current partner isn't right for you, be sure you have actually lived your script long enough to give them an opportunity to see the real soulful you. Be sure you have lived your script long enough to have been truthful about who you are and owned the unloving things you may have done in the past. Make sure you have put in the work to try to deeply understand them in an effort to connect and honor their potential. Do you really understand their pain, their struggles, and their obstacles to growth? Can you see the glorious soul in them as full of potential? Are you invested in the promise of their work and ready to be their workmate?

If after that process, you have to decide in truth to part ways, do that with compassion. But for some, living their beliefs will transform that old relationship into something that makes you both ready to be workmates.

I divorced and remarried, but without the benefit of living my beliefs in my first marriage. I didn't know how to do it and instead followed a similar pattern of subconsciously blaming my mate for my unhappy existence and stifled potential. I thought *he* was the obstacle to my peace and happiness, but it was *me*. Although I believe we weren't compatible in the long run, I certainly cannot tell you that for sure. My spiritual awakening came long after our relationship was over, so I know I was never a workmate to him.

Living in truth requires that I see the role I played in the painful and purpose-distracting divorce that ensued. Being remarried now, I get to see what a difference transformational love has on two imperfect people. It is hard to offer grace. It is hard to do the work to live your beliefs, but if you do, your workmate will be an invaluable asset to your life journey. They are closest to you so the light they can cast will help you wherever you are led to go.

There is so much more that can be said on this topic, but the key takeaways are that romantic upheaval is a significant distraction to your callings. Don't be quick to commit to relationships without careful assessment of workmate potential. And don't be quick to leave a relationship that could possibly thrive if you anchored your life in what you believe.

MY SUSTAINER

In closing, I would like to share a few thoughts on the person that sustained me long before I knew what a sustainer was and why I needed him to follow my work.

This person was my grandfather—James C. Swann. I miss him always, but the loss feels compounded on Father's Day. One year, I wondered what he might say to me if he had the chance to write me one last letter. I was writing a blog at the time and decided to try to write the letter to myself based on the actions and words he shared with me in life.

Many of these ideas inspired this book so I wanted to share them in closing in part to honor him, but also because I believe in the continuous circle of life. His role here on Earth is over. I'm still here acting out mine. His words started in me young and here they are many years after he is gone written on this page, perhaps to be read even after I am gone.

I cannot say what if any impact will come from my life's work, but I know for certain that this book is a product of his life's work.

These are the five things I think he would have written to me about how to live fulfilled. I know he would have wanted them shared with you.

- **Never think more highly of yourself than you ought to.**

  He said this often. It was part of his favorite religious scripture and something he clearly communicated to his family. He knew that by thinking we were better than others, we lost our connection to them. He encouraged me to grow in compassion and humility and was quick to correct me when I lost sight of that.

- **Never dim your light because it is too bright for others.**

   I was an opinionated and stubborn child. Unlike many adults, my grandfather found that side of my personality amusing. He wasn't hesitant to put me in my place, but he also wanted to make sure that I learned to make peace with my unique and natural traits. He encouraged me to accept myself. He would have wanted me to provide a safe place for others to be their true selves and to grow at their own pace.

- **Never settle for less than love.**

   Love is the climax of every story worth writing. He wanted me to know that I was worthy of love. He saw the beauty in the life within me, before I was able to see it myself. He believed in what I could grow into if I was bold enough to follow my path. He *wasn't* at all quiet at times when he felt I was accepting less from life than the standard he wanted for me. He gave me the nerve to feel worthy of love and to live in power. I know he would want to make sure I kept doing that.

- **We cannot "be good," we can only "do good."**

   He didn't see people as good or bad. He knew that everyone was a mix of both—including him.

So instead he worked to be a part of something larger than himself. He tried to live a life where the fruit of his best intentions would speak louder than his shortcomings. He didn't hide that he wasn't a perfect man, but he was always trying to grow. And he encouraged me to do the same. He knew that it was possible to transcend our imperfection through the pursuit of something bigger than us.

- **We are here to serve each other.**

  He believed this deeply. He saw service as our higher calling. He served in every aspect of his life from family to work. But most importantly to him, he served God. If he were able to write me this letter, I have no doubt that he would want to root me even deeper in my faith. He would encourage me to live my beliefs and to seek fulfillment through the work I do for others.

He spent many years of his life living in fulfillment. Certainly not his entire life—nobody gets to bypass the struggles and history that shape our callings. But he did the work to get past those stages and point his attention on something greater. He found several missions in his life and went to work serving them. It wasn't grand, and he was never famous, but he was fulfilled. He was loved.

Who knows what the full impact of his life's work was. I will never know exactly, but I do know that he followed his callings while he had a chance to. Now I get to keep following mine and you get to keep following yours.

ACKNOWLEDGMENTS

"Actions are the driving force that bring our highest work into fruition."

I need to thank several special individuals for directing their wisdom, gifts, and actions toward this book. Each one of you invested your precious time to bring it to life. *Working Whole* would not exist without you and I am forever grateful.

Andrea Upchurch—first reader, volunteer editor, and spiritual partner: I needed you every step of the way. You shaped the direction of this book with your thoughtful feedback. I hope you feel as much a part of the final outcome as I do.

Sandy Draper—editor and book-birthing coach: Words will never do justice to how much I came to rely on you. Your care and expertise helped create something above and beyond my abilities. You will be in my heart forever.

Sarah Beaudin—visual designer and publishing consultant: Thank you for sharing your enormous talent with me. You have a keen eye for design and the ability to effortlessly breathe beauty into the work of others. I'm inspired by you and the life you lead.

Liz Psaltis—marketing director: I cannot imagine going through the publishing process without you. I count you regularly as a miracle in my life. You showed up when I needed you most and allowed me to enjoy this amazing process. Thank you for that gift.

Madeleine Curry—proofreader: Your skill and attention to detail gave me a sense of comfort that you cannot fully appreciate. Thank you for your finishing touches.

Amanda, Rory, Micah and Steve—my mentors: Thank you for your encouragement and inspiration. But more i mportantly, thank you for the example you have set for me to be bold in my work and anchored in my beliefs. You are the courageous servant leaders I aim to be.

My parents, sons, grandmother, brother, cousin Tammie, and dear friends Tia and Courtney—my sustainers: Thank you for always supporting me, but especially during the last four years, your love has helped create this book.

Terrance—my husband and workmate: You cannot begin to understand how much I trust and respect you. Your life's work inspires me. Thank you for always having my back and helping me follow the work of my life.

ABOUT THE AUTHOR

Through her positions at top executive recruiting firms and consulting companies, **Kourtney Whitehead** has focused her career on helping people reach their work goals, from executive searches to counselling to career transitions. She holds a Master's degree in Education & Human Development from George Washington University and is a regular volunteer with high school and graduate-level students, advising them on careers and college, and sits on the board of the Children's Environmental Health Network.

Her site, SimplyService.org is an online community focused on supporting the creation of spiritually-centered work lives. Kourtney is a lover of trees, books, cozy blankets and unusual socks. She is a sought-after speaker and podcast guest and lives in the Washington, D.C. area with her husband and two sons.

Made in the USA
Middletown, DE
05 March 2019